# NORMS IN THE WILD

# NORMS
# IN THE WILD

*How to Diagnose, Measure,*
*and Change Social Norms*

CRISTINA BICCHIERI

OXFORD
UNIVERSITY PRESS

OXFORD
UNIVERSITY PRESS

Oxford University Press is a department of the University of Oxford. It furthers
the University's objective of excellence in research, scholarship, and education
by publishing worldwide. Oxford is a registered trade mark of Oxford University
Press in the UK and certain other countries.

Published in the United States of America by Oxford University Press
198 Madison Avenue, New York, NY 10016, United States of America.

Library of Congress Cataloging-in-Publication Data
Names: Bicchieri, Cristina, author.
Title: Norms in the wild : how to diagnose, measure, and change
   social norms / Cristina Bicchieri.
Description: New York, NY : Oxford University Press, [2017] |
   Includes bibliographical references.
Identifiers: LCCN 2016022291 | ISBN 9780190622046 (hbk : alk. paper) |
   ISBN 9780190622053 (pbk : alk. paper)
Subjects: LCSH: Collective behavior. | Behavior modification. |
   Social psychology. | Social norms.
Classification: LCC HM866 .B53 2017 | DDC 302.3/5—dc23
LC record available at https://lccn.loc.gov/2016022291

9  8  7

Paperback printed by Marquis, Canada
Hardback printed by Bridgeport National Bindery, Inc., United States of America

# CONTENTS

# PREFACE

In theory, there is no difference between theory and practice. In practice, there is.

*Yogi Berra*

I was invited, in November 2012, to present the Descartes lectures at the University of Tilburg. By that time, I had been deeply involved for a number of years in a project that aimed at integrating my theory of social norms with UNICEF's perspective on social change, and I decided to present on this experience. This book expands those three early lectures, but it retains the original flavor of a condensed attempt to spell out what norms are, how to measure and change them, and the theory and practical tools that lie beneath this project.

Many of the questions I ask and the answers I propose were motivated by discussions with field practitioners who wanted, above all, real-world guidance. I have tried to convince them, and my present readers, that such guidance is useless without an understanding of the ideas that motivate it, and of the theoretical tools that ground the choice of selecting and implementing practical interventions. What follows is a story of how my connection with people daily engaged in solving hard social problems and putting great effort into the discovery of practical, effective tools has opened my mind and helped me sharpen ideas that needed much clearing up to be used "in the wild."

It all started in the winter of 2008, when I was asked to give a talk at the UNICEF headquarters in New York. A few participants had read my 2006 book on social norms, and were interested in exploring possible applications of my social norms theory to violations of human rights across the world. I went in prepared to give an academic presentation, and I was pleasantly surprised to realize that the questions asked were not at all academic. The questions ranged from *"how can we tell that a common practice is a social norm?"* to *"what are the indicators we should use?"* and *"what does it mean to say that norms influence behavior?"* These novel questions forced me to think hard about the possible applications of my ideas on social norms to real-life cases.

When I mentioned the importance of social expectations in identifying norms, my audience was eager to understand the difference between expectations of how other people will behave in specific situations (*empirical expectations*) and expectations about what other people think one should do in those situations (*normative expectations*). This distinction is important, and not well understood in the social norms literature, which typically stresses the actions usually or "normally" performed by people, the personal attitudes they have toward such actions, and the social sanctions that may follow transgressions, but not the conditions that make these actions normal, the application of measures of attitudes, and when these sanctions are relevant. What we interpret "from the outside" as usual behavior may or may not be conceived by the actors themselves as normal and usual. Sanctions have value only if they are expected by their targets, and the concept of attitude is too general to be very useful in measuring normative behavior.

Introducing the idea of social expectations has several advantages. Not only does it ground behavior on the actual beliefs of actors, but also lets us take the presence or absence of expectations as indicators of different collective behaviors. Measuring social expectations, and their influence on behavior, allows us to identify different types of collective behaviors that may otherwise be confused. Think of child marriage: is it a custom, a social norm, a simple convention, a response to the moral imperative of protecting one's child, or a reaction to difficult economic conditions? We may observe identical behaviors, but the reasons behind them may significantly vary. Indeed, the same actions may be independent or interdependent, and interventions aimed at successfully changing behavior must first understand the nature of the collective behavior in question.

Another advantage of employing social expectations is that they are easily measurable. We can always tell if they exist. Yet it is not enough to assess that expectations exist. For a social norm to exist, social expectations must *matter*. Our choices, in other words, must be influenced by our having expectations about what others do and think we should do. Measurement, again, is important in determining if and how much expectations matter, and whether some matter more than others. Norms have causal power, and measurement helps identify the ways in which they influence behavior.

My original audience agreed with the idea that people follow social norms because they have expectations about how others behave and what they consider appropriate. Yet the apparently simple idea of *conditional preference* raised a host of new questions. *"If one prefers to do something because one expects friends and neighbors to do the same, what motivates this preference?" "Is it imitation, the desire to coordinate with others, or fear of being judged and punished if we behave differently?"* *"How can we tell the difference?"* These questions are practical ones: If people do something because they want to imitate the powerful or the successful, then, to change the followers' behavior, it may be sufficient to persuade reputable leaders to embrace new behaviors. If instead people want to coordinate their actions, we need to create new ways to coordinate on a better outcome, a task significantly more difficult than changing the opinions of one or two leaders. Moreover, while an imitator's choice to adopt or ignore a behavior carries no consequence, the presence of a social norm encouraging or discouraging the same behavior can include consequential sanctions to prevent the violation of that norm. Measuring whether expectations exist, and whether they matter to choice, helps us correctly diagnose what sort of collective behavior we are facing.

Correct diagnosis of the nature of a collective behavior is necessary, but not sufficient, to decide how to intervene if change is desired. When I was first writing about social norms, I wanted to find a way to differentiate various types of collective behaviors, and I was not unduly worried about practical applications, even if my definition did provide an operational meaning to the concept of social norm. My goal at the time was to test this concept and its consequences in behavioral experiments, check if behaviors such as cooperation, fairness, and reciprocity are norm-driven, and if influencing expectations would change behaviors in predictable directions. I succeeded in measuring expectations and showing how "manipulating" them changes behavior, sometimes quite dramatically. For example, manipulating information about whether the majority of participants in earlier experiments equally shared with their partner the money they received significantly changes how new participants expect other participants to behave and how they themselves distribute the money. Yet the lab is not the field, and inducing different expectations "in the wild" turns out to be a task fraught with difficulties, since we cannot easily manipulate expectations as we do in the lab. To change expectations in the field, people must have good evidence that those who matter to them have changed behavior, and so no longer condemn certain actions. Expectations change when collective behavior changes, and promoting behavioral change, even if just in a slice of population, is a daunting task.

Over the years, considering specific and very concrete problems has changed and refined my views about the dynamics of social norms. The examples range from human rights violations—in particular, instances of child marriage, female genital cutting, and gender violence—to matters of health care and sanitation. How to set up successful AIDS campaigns, convince mothers to nurse their children from birth, or induce people to build and use latrines are practical and intellectual challenges. I will explain that to effectively challenge norms that deny what we consider to be fundamental human rights, we must understand what sort of reasons would induce behavioral change, and what drives belief revision in cultures profoundly different from ours, whose ways of evaluating evidence lead to conclusions that we would normally reject.

Talking over the years to UNICEF and workers in nongovernmental organizations (NGOs) has often been a challenge, but a fruitful one nonetheless. As a theorist, I seldom think of the practical impact of my ideas and models, and how to apply them to real-life situations. My close collaboration with non-academic groups taught me that ideas that seemed completely clear, at least conceptually, needed much more fine-tuning if I wanted to use them to explain, for example, why people marry off their daughters when they are still children, why there are pockets of resistance to polio vaccination in several parts of the world, or, more generally, why some interventions are very successful whereas others fail. In many instances, we can see that a range of external factors converge to produce particular collective behaviors. Economic and ecological conditions matter, as do political and social circumstances. Often missing from an analysis of these factors is a consideration of how social norms shape collective behaviors and what an important tool for change they may become.

Norms and values often support behaviors that we would like to alter, as change would help people to live better, healthier lives and develop their full potentials. Open discussions about sexuality, relationships, and sexual behaviors have conventionally been taboo in many parts of the world where AIDS is endemic. Traditional gender roles and their accompanying norms may prevent successful interventions: there are many things a decent man would not do in many parts of Africa. Accompanying his wife to the market is one, and attending a health clinic is another. Information campaigns that fail to consider these social hurdles are often ineffective in changing behavior, and legislation that is far from what is customary and widely accepted is bound to fail. Since many behaviors that we may want to change are interdependent, in that they are driven by social expectations, targeting individuals in isolation is also destined to fail. I will argue that identifying social expectations plays a crucial role in considering these social hurdles and consequently challenging maladaptive norms.

Changing social norms involves changing preferences, beliefs, and social expectations, but where is a good point to start? How a negative norm may be abandoned, and how a positive new norm may be created, have been recurring themes in the search for solutions to a host of disparate cases. Identifying norms that may need change is just the beginning. After correctly identifying the nature of the current social practice, we must determine which means to use to effect change. A norm that is part of a village culture is very different from a norm that is adopted in a much larger environment, such as a big city. Villages typically have thick networks of relations. Networks in cities are much less dense, and a person may belong to many networks at the same time. Size matters to the type of intervention employed. Collective discussions may do wonders in small groups, but what about in large, anonymous environments? I will discuss the tools we may use in different environments, and how they may be combined to maximum efficacy.

In both the creation and abandonment of social norms, expectations matter. But what sort of expectations matter the most? Is it empirical or normative expectations that take precedence? Sometimes, people must see that others behave differently to start exploring new ways of doing things themselves. In this case, their empirical expectations must change first. Knowing that many others have changed behavior may, in time, convince actors that no punishment will follow if they do the same, consequently changing their normative expectations. At other times, especially when a new norm is emerging, agreed-upon sanctions will tell people that the old behavior is no longer approved and should be abandoned. In this case, new normative expectations are the first hint that change is coming. When those who are expected to engage in the newly approved behavior start conforming to it, new empirical expectations are created.

The conditions by which expectations may change vary: there are many different means we can adopt to promote change, depending on the social ecology of the targeted community. The size of the affected group is important, as well as who shares significant connections within the group. People do not make choices in isolation: they pay attention to what other people do, and what others approve or disapprove of. But who are these other people that individuals observe before acting themselves? In other words, who belongs to each person's main reference network? We must be aware that, within a network, some people are more influential or trusted than others. I will explain how the influence of reference networks is critical to understanding the dynamics of change.

An important element of norm creation or change is the dynamic of mutual expectations. Changing empirical expectations is easy in the case of public practices (as people learn from observing and communicating with others), but not all practices are visible. Norms that regulate private behaviors (such as sexuality) are particularly difficult to change since other people's behavior is not usually observed. We may adopt a norm that prohibits premarital sex, but can only observe the consequences of violations (out of wedlock pregnancies). If there is a high rate of secret abortions, we may still believe that the norm is obeyed, when in fact it is not. Empirical expectations in this case would not change, as there would be no learning.

Normative expectations are usually much harder to change alone, without an antecedent change in empirical expectations. If a norm is well established, sanctions for misbehaving are to be expected, and usually we do not witness deviations. Often, normative expectations are not explicitly stated, but are inferred from behavior, as when observing widespread compliance with a norm leads us to believe that everyone supports it. The reality may be quite different, as real and perceived support may be at odds. If it is not possible to openly communicate what we really think about the norm we all seem to uphold, the presumed link between empirical (all do it) and normative (all approve of it) expectations may lead us into epistemic traps that are difficult to escape. Bad norms often survive for this reason.

As I mentioned above, changing empirical expectations is easy so long as individuals can observe enough other people adopting a different behavior. This observation can also be crucial to the subsequent change of normative expectations and the eventual abandonment of a social norm. The problem is that we may never witness different behavior! When a social norm is in place, individuals fear that deviations will be punished, and they are often right. So who will be the first to deviate? Any study of social norm dynamics has to answer this crucial question. History and experience teach us that, with every norm change, there are always "first movers" or trendsetters, people who defy convention and spearhead new behaviors. Who are these trendsetters? It depends on the situation. Someone may be a trendsetter in abandoning a norm of child marriage, but be very conservative with respect to gender norms. Trendsetters may have general traits, such as high levels of perceived autonomy and self-efficacy. I will argue that the most important traits for norm change are a low sensitivity to the target norm and the subjective perception that one may not risk much by deviating from it. As we shall see, those who start to move away from an established norm are often at the periphery of a network, whereas those who try to introduce a new norm are often more central.

Social expectations and conditional preferences, again, are important to identify trendsetters. When we measure if and how much social expectations matter to an individual's choice, we can easily determine how sensitive that individual is to a specific norm, and whether her risk perception is high or low. Identifying trendsetters with the methods I describe throughout the book, in addition to recognizing and understanding the different motivations underlying interdependent and independent behaviors, is essential to promoting successful behavioral change.

The remainder of this book will draw on the crucial part social expectations and conditional preferences play in identifying types of collective behaviors, diagnosing the presence of norms, and shaping the means we can successfully apply to encourage both the abandonment of old norms and the implementation of new norms in their place. The wild is real life, where theory and practice meet, synergies are created, and changes occur.

# ACKNOWLEDGMENTS

This book started as the three Descartes lectures I was invited to present at the University of Tilburg in November 2012. I wish to thank Stephan Hartmann, who organized the lectures, and my three commentators, Jerry Gaus, Ken Binmore, and Francesco Guala for their thoughtful comments and pleasant company in Tilburg. These initial lectures were refined and expanded as I presented the material in the following years to academic and non-academic audiences. Some of the topics I discuss became part of my Silver Jubilee Lectures at the Indira Gandhi Institute of Development Research in Mumbai in 2013; others were presented as the Pufendorf Lectures I gave at Lund University in 2015. The audiences at these lectures were full of comments and great insights. In particular, I wish to thank S. Mahendra Dev, P. G. Babu, Sarkar Jayati, Peter Gardenfors, Bjorn Petersson, Ingar Brink, Eric Olsson, Carlo Proietti, and Tom Persson for fruitful discussions and suggestions.

Many of the examples I present have been inspired by the interactions with participants at the Penn-UNICEF program on Social Norms and Social Change, which started in 2010 and is ongoing. I learned a lot from all the participants, who came to Penn with very real problems they wanted to understand. Therese Dooley and Otniel Habila taught me about sanitation and the CATS program; from Felicite Tchibindad I learned about breastfeeding and the power of mothers-in-law; Joachim Thiel explained to me why sometimes child marriage is not a social norm but is supported by many; Molly Melching convinced me of the importance of the group discussions Tostan introduced; and from Antanas Mockus I learned how we could be creative in designing interventions aimed at changing long-standing bad behaviors.

The presentation of ideas in this book was affected, in a good way, by a number of people. Alessandro Sontuoso, Ryan Muldoon, Rosemarie Nagel, Sebastiano Bavetta, Massimo Bigliardo, Jan Willem Lindemans, Ting Jiang, Jon Baron, Barbara Mellers, my students Thomas Noah, Molly Sinderbrand, Javier Guillot, Marie Barnett, Raj Patel, and Erik Thulin, and the participants in our BeLab weekly seminars provided insightful feedback on earlier versions of some chapters of this manuscript. I also benefited from fantastic editorial help. Peter McNally, my former research assistant, made my sentences better, suggested changes when changes were needed, and was always ready to discuss with me every idea I was willing to throw at him. His help was invaluable. Jayson Dorset, my new research assistant, came in time to proofread the entire manuscript, and added clarity to my message. Finally, I wish to thank Daniele Bigliardo for designing the book cover, converting into art my ideas about trendsetters.

My work, especially the part that analyzes trendsetters and their characteristics, was supported by a grant from the Templeton Foundation to explore the link between autonomy and liberalism. I have focused on autonomy as one of the drivers of social change, and identified trendsetters as crucial first movers in a process of change that, under certain conditions, can move society to a better political and economic state.

# DIAGNOSING NORMS

We often find ourselves wondering how social practices that cause societal damage, violate human rights, or are plainly inefficient can survive. Think of how corruption holds back economic development, erodes public confidence in government, and undermines the rule of law and fair competition, or how child marriage forces girls out of education and into a life of increased risk of violence, abuse, ill health, or even early death. What motivates such behaviors, and why do they persist, even in the face of laws that prohibit them? Are these practices supported by cultural norms? How do economic and cultural structures interact? Which of these questions is most important to address? Understanding the nature of collective behaviors and why people engage in them is critical for the design of appropriate interventions aimed at social change. There are many collective behaviors that are maladaptive, harmful, or violate what we take to be basic human rights. Addressing these behaviors requires disentangling the personal, social, economic, and cultural factors that support them and assessing their relative weights in sustaining these practices.

Collective behaviors, that is, behavioral patterns shared by a group of individuals, may be studied in a variety of ways. For example, we may explore the functions they perform in a society or group and investigate the environments within which they emerge or disappear. Knowing the functions a practice performs, however, does not tell us if those involved in it are aware of them, or if they act in certain ways *because* of them. We should not make the mistake of conflating the observer's and the actor's points of view. We may think that a social norm maximizes the welfare of its followers, but this may hardly be the reason why they conform to it. Most of the time, participants are not aware of the social functions that a practice serves. Alternatively, we may focus on the reasons why people engage in such behaviors by investigating the incentives and constraints that they face when undertaking an established behavior or adopting a new one. These two approaches are fully compatible, and the importance of stressing one or the other depends upon our intellectual and practical goals. Especially when wanting to change or promote a particular collective behavior, we must understand its nature and the reasons why people take part in it.

In this chapter, I will distinguish between collective behaviors that are completely *independent*, as when they are purely determined by economic or natural reasons, and *interdependent*, as when other people's actions and opinions matter to one's choice.[1] I want to differentiate actions that are undertaken because we care about what other people do or think from actions that we have reason to carry out without regard for other people's behavior or beliefs. These distinctions are important because in order to implement policies to encourage or discourage certain collective behaviors or practices, we need to understand their nature, or the reasons why people engage in them. In what follows, I shall offer a clear and simple way to distinguish between independent and interdependent behaviors and among different types of interdependent behaviors.

Habits, social customs, and moral injunctions are independent, in the sense that they involve undertaking certain actions regardless of what others do or expect us to do. For

1. When I say "independence," I do not refer to outcome-independence: in a purely competitive market, each agent acts independently, but the final outcome is the product of a myriad of individual choices. The market outcome *depends* on the actions of all the market participants, but this is not the dependence I am interested in.

example, we wear warm clothes in winter and use umbrellas when it rains, independently of what our friends or neighbors do, and we may obey kashrut dietary laws whether or not other Jews respect them. Conventions such as signaling systems, fads, fashions, and social norms such as reciprocity rules are all interdependent behaviors, and social norms are the foremost example of interdependence. However, as I will make clear later on, not all collective behaviors are interdependent, and not all interdependent behaviors are social norms.

This chapter draws on Bicchieri 2006, ch. 1, although some of the details provided here are different from those in the book. Here my aim is to offer simple tools that help to quickly decide whether the collective behavior we care about is a norm or more simply a shared custom, and if it is a norm, what sort of norm it is. Without this knowledge, promoting social change would be difficult, as we would be at a loss about where and how to intervene. The same practice could be a custom, a convention, or a social norm in different populations. Being able to determine why it is followed will help us suggest the most appropriate intervention. In what follows I shall rely on concepts such as expectations and preferences, all of which are relatively easy to measure and handle, especially in light of wanting to conduct experiments or field surveys. *How* we come to the conclusion that a collective behavior is a social norm is the subject of the next chapter, where I will discuss ways to measure norms that are based on the concepts introduced here.

Here I shall offer a few static definitions. They are *static* because in real life, the social constructs I talk about may morph into each other and often do. A custom may become a social norm in time, and a social norm may revert to a custom (think of the use of white wedding dresses). This dynamic process merits investigation, but for the moment I will be treating social constructs as separate, fixed entities. This classification will help us diagnose the nature of a practice or action pattern, in turn suggesting the best way to encourage or discourage it.

*How* individuals relate to certain patterns of behavior determines the pattern's nature. There are highways where most people drive over the speed limit, precincts with low voter turnout, pockets of resistance to polio vaccination, littered environments, countries where bribing is endemic, and cultures where girls are married at a very young age. What drives these behaviors? Are choices independent or interdependent? Understanding the motives behind these collective behaviors is critical to changing them.

Diagnosing collective patterns of behavior as interdependent, and being very specific about the nature of this interdependence, will help us decide what sort of intervention offers the best chance of success. Think of widespread HIV awareness campaigns in African countries, where condoms are freely distributed to the population, yet the number of newly infected people is increasing. Distributing condoms and relying on information campaigns about the risks of unprotected sex is insufficient if men share a common view of masculinity that glorifies promiscuity and if they refrain from using condoms at home for fear of giving away the existence of "other women." When behaviors are interdependent, we have to consider entire communities, as individuals' choices depend on what people who are important to them do, and possibly also on what they judge appropriate or inappropriate.

Think of child marriage, an interdependent practice that many governments and international organizations are actively trying to eliminate. According to the International Center for Research on Women (ICRW), 100 million girls will be married before the age of eighteen in the coming decade. Most live in sub-Saharan Africa and the Asian Subcontinent. A variety of potential causes have been explored. The parents of child brides are often poor and use marriage as a way to provide for their daughter's future, especially in areas where there are few economic opportunities for women. Some families use marriage to build and strengthen alliances, to seal property deals, settle disputes, or pay off debts. In some cultures, child marriage is encouraged to increase the number of pregnancies and ensure enough children survive into adulthood to work on family land and support elderly relatives. In South Asia, some families marry off all their daughters at the same time to reduce the cost of the wedding ceremony. Chastity and family honor are another major reason, as many parents want to make sure their daughters do not have a child out-of-wedlock (Bicchieri, Lindemans, and Jiang 2014).

There are a variety of cultural reasons for child marriage, but in most cases, the social pressure to marry very young girls is intense. In India's southern state of Tamil Nadu, some communities have a strong social stigma against girls being married after puberty. Often African families report fearing that if girls receive an education, they will be less willing to fulfill their traditional roles as wife and mother, and so it will be difficult for them to find a husband, with negative consequences for the family. Trying to induce a change in behavior critically depends upon understanding the reasons behind the choices. In many cases such choices are driven by a combination of shared factual beliefs (about the value of education and how best to protect a girl), social expectations (what other families do and think is appropriate), and normative (or religious) constraints (what good parents should do).

Let us imagine two separate groups who marry their daughters as soon as they reach puberty. These practices look identical, but the beliefs supporting them are very different, and these differences have major consequences for policies aimed at curbing the practice. Members of the first group believe their religion calls for early marriage, and deviating from a religious injunction will bring disgrace to the entire family. They may entertain a host of other beliefs about marriage: they may believe that a young bride is more valuable, more fertile, more likely to obey her in-laws, will be protected from sexual violence or out-of-wedlock births that would dishonor the family, and so on. The members of the second group have similar beliefs, but lack the religious principle that fosters the first group's practice. In both cases, the social pressure to marry young girls will be intense, but within the first group the religious beliefs will represent a major stumbling block to changing marriage practices. We may work hard to change some factual beliefs in both groups, and possibly succeed. We may build safe schools for girls, and help appease fears of violence and dishonor, pay parents for attendance and subsequently provide jobs to the girls, but the unconditional allegiance to a religious creed will be much harder to overcome. I will explore the factors that differentiate these two groups—which would inform the design of policies aiming at changing these practices—in a later section of this chapter.

## CONDITIONAL PREFERENCES

In what follows I offer a simple way to discriminate between behavioral patterns shared by a group. The concepts I use to this effect are those of *preference* and *expectation*. Preferences are dispositions to act in a particular way in a specific situation. When I say that I prefer to drive to school instead of taking the train, I mean that, if given the choice, I would take the car. Often people make the mistake of equating preference with "liking better." If I choose a vanilla ice cream instead of a chocolate one, you may infer that I like vanilla better. What you may not know is that I adore chocolate but am allergic to it. So despite liking chocolate more, I prefer (choose) vanilla instead. What preference really means is that, in a choice situation, if

I choose A over B it must be the case that, *all things considered*, I prefer A. Preference and choice are thus strictly connected.

Preferences may be strictly individual (like the ice cream example), or they may be social. For example, I may not eat ice cream when I am out with friends since they have passionate views about dieting. Social preferences may take into account the behavior, beliefs, and outcomes of other people that, presumably, matter to the decision maker. Some such preferences are consequentialist, in that the decision maker only cares about the final outcome, not how it was obtained, nor whether the other parties had expectations about his or her choice. Say you have a preference for fair divisions. Then, if you have to choose how to allocate some good, you will take into account how much of it goes to other claimants, and you may feel guilty if you take too much for yourself. Alternatively, you may be envious and resent an allocation that grants a larger share to others, or you might even be spiteful and want to maximize the difference between what you and others receive. In all of these cases, you care about what you get *and* what others get, too. You make social comparisons, but you may not be concerned about what the other parties do or believe, or how the outcome came about. Your only concern is how the final outcome is allocated. So someone who decides to split a sum of money into equal parts may be moved by an independent desire to be fair, or instead she may respond to what she believes is expected of her. In both cases we say that she has a *social preference*, though she might be influenced either by a social comparison or by social expectations.

Social preferences that are based on social comparisons can be *unconditional*, in that one's choice is not influenced by knowing how others act in similar situations or what they approve/disapprove of. If instead one chooses an action based on expectations about what others do or believe should be done, then such preferences are *conditional* on those actions and beliefs. For example, a mother may choose to overtly beat her child because all the other parents around her do so, and she fears being looked down upon or reprimanded if she does not hit him hard. In fact, she might not like to punish so harshly, but what would the neighbors think of her? In this case, we say that her "preference" for corporal punishment is conditional upon her social expectations. She chooses to hit because she sees other parents hitting, and she believes that she would suffer negative consequences if she behaved differently and her behavior could be detected. Saying that she has a social preference for beating her disobedient child does not tell us whether her preference is unconditional, that is, she is genuinely convinced about the merits of corporal punishment, or is conditional, in that she is influenced by what her neighbors think and do.

Returning to the case of fair division, you may not care at all about fairness per se, but you nevertheless divide the good equally because you are sensitive to what others normally do and expect you to do. In other words, you have a preference for sharing conditional on the fact that others share. This is quite different from being independently motivated to act fairly. The social preferences I will be talking about are mostly conditional, in the sense that the behaviors of interest often depend on what other people that matter to the actor think and do. Interdependent actions, as we shall see, always involve socially conditional preferences.[2] Table 1.1 describes different kinds of preferences, using the simple example of preferring or not preferring to eat apples.

Preferences should not be confused with what social psychologists call "attitudes" (Fishbein 1967). An *attitude* is understood as an evaluative disposition toward some object, person,

---

2. From now on, when I talk of conditional preferences, I always mean "socially" conditional preferences.

Table 1.1

### CLASSIFYING DIFFERENT TYPES OF PREFERENCES

|  | Individual preferences | Social preferences |
|---|---|---|
| Unconditional | "I want apples." | "I want more apples than you." |
| Conditional | "I want apples if it is autumn." | "I want apples if my friends want apples." |

or behavior. It can be expressed by statements such as "I like/ dislike," "I believe one should/should not," and "I approve/dis-approve of." Attitudes thus include *personal* normative beliefs that express a person's positive or negative evaluation of particular behaviors. Such personal normative beliefs, in turn, can be prudential, or they can have a "moral"[3] motivation. I may disapprove of smoking in a prudential sense because I know its negative health effects. In other words, I believe that smoking is inadvisable or not in one's best interest. Historically, smoking by women was strongly disapproved in a moral sense in that it was seen as a sign of debauchery and lack of womanly virtues. Such a moral personal normative belief implies that one's ethical convictions motivate disapproval. I shall return to this point in the next section.

We know from economics that preferences and choices are positively correlated. What about attitudes and choices? We might expect that people who positively evaluate a particular behavior would engage in the behavior to a greater degree than others might. If a group of people thinks that drinking alcohol is acceptable, should we not witness a lot of drinking in this

---

3. Here and elsewhere, I use "moral" in the broad sense of the term, as referring to certain codes of conduct adopted by an individual, a group or a society.

population? Unfortunately, it has been consistently observed that general attitudes and behavior are weakly correlated, if they are correlated at all (Wicker 1969).[4] Individuals may express positive judgments toward behaviors that they nevertheless do not engage in. Why so? To answer, consider that most of our choices are not made in a vacuum. We are social animals embedded in thick networks of relations, and what we do has consequences, for us and for others. Interdependence, not independence, rules social life. Indeed, a host of studies show that the main variable affecting behavior is not what one personally likes or thinks he should do, but rather one's belief about what "society" (i.e., most other people, people who matter to us, and the like) approves of (see, e.g., Bicchieri and Muldoon 2011; Fishbein 1967).

A woman might *prefer* not to breastfeed after giving birth, even if she has learned about the advantages of feeding colostrum to the baby, or a family might *prefer* to give their young daughter in marriage even if they would have liked it better to send her to school and wait. These choices occur regardless of the mother or family's attitudes toward these practices. All these preferences are conditional on expecting people who matter to us to do the same, approve of such behaviors, and possibly punish deviations. Having a conditional preference implies that one may have a reason to avoid early breastfeeding or marry off one's child, which is different from liking and endorsing these practices. To uncover the reasons why a collective behavior survives, we have to look beyond attitudes to the beliefs and conditional preferences of those who engage in it. This is why I like to use almost exclusively preferences and expectations in

4. However, when there is a high level of correspondence between an attitude and a behavior, then attitudes can be predictive of behaviors; see Ajzen and Fishbein 1977.

my analysis of norms. They are easy to measure, and measuring them lets us meaningfully classify collective behaviors.

## SOCIAL EXPECTATIONS

People who have conditional social preferences care about what others who matter to them do and/or approve of. They have expectations that influence their behavior (Bicchieri 2014). A driver will stop on red and go on green because she has expectations about how other drivers will behave and how they expect her to behave. A parent who beats a child will have expectations about what other parents in his neighborhood do, and how they may judge him. These *expectations* are just beliefs. We have all sorts of beliefs. We believe that tomorrow it will rain, and we believe that people drive faster on I-96 than the speed limit and are hardly monitored. Beliefs can be factual or they can be normative. Both "I believe that colostrum is dirty and dangerous for the baby" and "I believe that dowry costs increase with the bride's age" are *factual* beliefs, beliefs about states of affairs, though only one is true. As we shall see later on, belief change is an important part of social change. People need *reasons* to change, and realizing that some of their factual beliefs are false can give them the needed push to consider alternatives. Beliefs like "women should cover their heads and faces" are instead *normative,* in that the "should" expresses an evaluation—it signals approval of veiling women.

Expectations are beliefs about what is going to happen or what should happen; both presuppose a continuity between past and present or future. In what follows, I will only refer to *social expectations,* that is, the expectations we have about other people's behaviors and beliefs. Some social expectations are factual or empirical: they are beliefs about how other people are going to act or react in certain situations. We may have observed how people behave, or some trusted source may have told us that people behave in such and such a way. If we have reason to believe that they will continue to act as in the past, we will have formed empirical expectations about their future behavior. What matters to our analysis is that very often these *empirical expectations influence our decisions*. For example, if every time I go to England I observe people driving on the left side of the road, and I have no reason to think there has been a change, I will expect left-side driving the next time around. Wanting to avoid an accident, I will drive on the left side, too.

Other social expectations are normative, in that they express our belief that other people believe (and will continue to believe) that certain behaviors are praiseworthy and should be carried out, while others should be avoided. *Normative (social) expectations are beliefs about other people's personal normative beliefs* (i.e., they are second-order beliefs). "I believe that the women in my village believe that a good mother should abstain from nursing her newborn baby" is a normative expectation, and it may have a powerful influence on behavior. Table 1.2 exemplifies the important differences between different types of beliefs.

### Table 1.2

## CLASSIFICATION OF NORMATIVE/NON-NORMATIVE AND SOCIAL/NON-SOCIAL BELIEFS

|  | *Non-social beliefs* | *Social beliefs* |
| --- | --- | --- |
| Non-normative beliefs | Factual beliefs | Empirical expectations |
| Normative beliefs | Personal normative beliefs | Normative expectations |

Important distinctions among personal normative beliefs are often missed in surveys, because questions about attitudes are often too vague to capture these distinctions. Attitude questions can include questions about personal normative beliefs, but no distinction is made between prudential versus "moral" normative beliefs. It is important to recognize the difference between different types of normativity. For example, a survey may pose questions like "do you believe that a wife should refrain from committing adultery?"; all the researcher attains with such questions are just the nonspecific personal normative beliefs of the responder.[5] Say two people, Anan and Dayo, both answer "yes" to the first question. Anan thinks that adultery always ultimately gets discovered, and the adulterer would be wise to renounce carnal temptations to avoid punishment, so her answer reflects a prudential "should." Dayo's answer instead reflects her judgment about adultery as a reprehensible breach of faith and trust in a marriage, regardless of the social consequences such actions incur. Dayo's "should" has a different, strongly normative connotation. How would new information change their minds? Given an environment in which adultery is tolerated or reliably undetectable, Anan could easily change her mind, but Dayo would not be swayed in her conviction about the ills of adultery. I shall discuss the difficulties involved in belief change in chapter 3.

Personal normative beliefs may or may not coincide with one's normative expectations. A woman may believe that she ought to infibulate her daughter, or she may be less sanguine about infibulation, and in both cases believe that her fellow villagers think she *ought* to infibulate her child. If she is obeying her group's norm to infibulate the child, regardless of her

---

5. I am for the moment assuming that the responder is sincere and a social desirability bias has been avoided. As we shall see in chapter 2, this assumption is often wrong.

personal normative beliefs, her behavior will be influenced by her beliefs about what relevant others think she should do— that is, her normative expectations. Notice that normative expectations always express an indirect evaluation: one believes that other people think one *ought* to behave in a certain way (or refrain from behaving in a certain way), where the *ought*, as we shall see, is not merely prudent. The man who beats his wife may believe that his neighbors approve of such behavior, that they think he should chastise her if she misbehaves. Again, this expectation presupposes some continuity between what was approved/disapproved in the past and what is approved/disapproved now and in the future.

But whose actions or approval do we care about? Depending on the circumstances, different people will matter to our decisions. They may be family members, clan or village members, religious authorities, co-workers, bystanders, and whoever in that moment has the power to influence our choice. What we expect them to do matters; what we think they believe we ought to do matters. I call the range of people whom we care about when making particular decisions our *reference network* because they may be spread around and not be physically present. The Pakistani man who killed his "dishonored" daughter in Milan, where he had lived for twenty years, was only concerned with the strict honor code of the relatives and friends in his Pakistani village. That was his reference network, not his Italian co-workers or neighbors. In Brazil, favela dwellers only punish stealing within their group, not stealing outside their group, so an action that is prohibited within a reference network may be permissible outside of it. It is important to keep in mind that a crucial element of any empirical study of social norms will be the identification of the reference network against which expectations are set.

For the time being, let us agree that there are two types of social expectations, empirical and normative, that they involve a reference network, and often, alone or in combination, influence our behavior. Let us now see what might be the relation between preferences, expectations, and patterns of behavior.

## CUSTOMS

Imagine observing a common pattern of behavior: when it rains, we see that people normally use umbrellas. Do they use umbrellas because other people do? Are their choices influenced by social expectations? If so, which expectations matter? Would they use umbrellas irrespective of what others do? These are questions we should ask if we want to diagnose the nature of collective behaviors.

Like using umbrellas when it rains, certain action patterns are created and sustained by the motivations of actors acting independently. Suppose you live in an environment where water is scarce and latrines do not exist. All find it useful to satisfy their bodily needs by defecating in the open. This action meets their needs and will therefore be repeated. This repetition will create a habit. Since people have similar needs, the habitual action that meets their needs will become a *custom*. The consistency of the pattern is due to the actors' similar motivations and conditions. Each actor acts independently, and the result is an emergent pattern of behavior that reproduces itself. Each individual knows that everybody else in her community acts in a similar way, but this awareness does not serve as a motive for doing what one does anyway, out of sheer need or convenience. As we shall see later on, these motives may act as drags on social change. I thus define a custom as follows:

> A custom is a pattern of behavior such that individuals (unconditionally) prefer to conform to it because it meets their needs.

Clearly, in the case of customs, preferences are unconditional. Expecting other people to behave in a similar way does not influence one's behavior, since this expectation is not a reason to persist in or change one's habit. We know that other people use umbrellas, but so what? Whatever they do, we will keep using our umbrellas when it rains!

Not all customs are benign, though they may efficiently serve some basic needs. Open defecation is an example of a custom that presents a huge sanitation problem in many parts of the world. It is estimated that 15 percent of the world population practices open defecation, with extremely negative health consequences, as well as social costs that are less easy to quantify.[6]

Customs can change in several ways. We may discover alternative, better means to satisfy our needs, the external conditions that produce these needs may cease to exist, new preferences may be created, or a combination of such changes may come about. Sometimes we come to grasp the advantages of new behaviors, but if there are costs involved, change may be hard to come by. This difficulty is due to the fact that the proposed alternative often requires collective action. The collective custom is a pattern of independent actions, but changing it introduces interdependencies. For example, abandoning open defecation requires first a change in factual beliefs about the health and social costs of this practice. The next step consists in building latrines, using them, and maintaining

6.  The majority of those practicing open defecation live in rural areas. Open defecation in rural areas persists in every region of the developing world, even among those who have otherwise reached high levels of improved sanitation use. For instance, the proportion of rural dwellers still practicing open defecation is 9 percent in Northern Africa and 17 percent in Latin America and the Caribbean. Open defecation is highest in rural areas of Southern Asia, where it is practiced by 55 percent of the population.

them operational. This process requires the engagement of the whole community, which has to allocate tasks and ensure that the old ways are abandoned; otherwise the health benefits of having functioning latrines may be lost. Here the individual incentive to continue with the established habit may conflict with the collective benefit of having better sanitation. People facing change confront a *social dilemma*: it is individually tempting (and most convenient) to stick to the old habit, but everyone would benefit from a collective shift to latrines. Yet if only some use latrines, the sanitation benefit is lost: water and land pollution will still occur. In this case, not only would everyone have to be convinced to change their ways, but the new behavior, in order to survive, would have to be supported by both the expectation that others are engaging in it and the expectation that most people think that the behavior should be followed. Such expectations played no role in the custom's survival, but they become critical for its demise.

What matters for the present discussion is that a *collective* process of belief change may be necessary to implement a new pattern of behavior, even when abandoning simple customs, especially if the new behavior requires the collaboration of everyone to be sustained. Collective belief change may not be sufficient in all those cases in which carrying out the new behavior involves a social dilemma. In cases of open defecation, building and maintaining latrines requires a collective effort and the introduction of sanctions to ensure continuous compliance, since even a few defectors can have a powerfully detrimental effect on a group's hygiene. Therefore monitoring adherence to the new behavior becomes all the more critical. Yet the introduction of sanctions, though crucial, is secondary to the initial process of factual belief change. People must first recognize the negative consequences of open defecation. How customs can be changed, and the challenges of sustaining new behaviors, is a topic I will discuss in the third chapter.

## DESCRIPTIVE NORMS

There are many collective behaviors that may look like customs but are instead influenced by social expectations. These collective behaviors depend on expectations about what others do or expect one to do in a similar situation. Such behaviors display various degrees of interdependence, depending on whether expectations are normative or empirical, unilateral or multilateral. I use the word *descriptive norm* to refer to all those interdependent behaviors where preferences are conditional on empirical expectations alone.

Let me add a note of warning, since my definition is unconventional. The term "descriptive norm" is widely employed to mean "what is commonly done," what is usual and customary (Schultz et al. 2007). It describes how people typically act, what they regularly do in particular situations. I find this definition too vague and of little practical use. The traditional understanding of a descriptive norm includes, for example, a custom like open defecation, a fashion like wearing high heels, or the use of a common signaling system, like traffic lights or language, for coordination purposes.

While the perceived existence of a custom alone does not cause people to engage in it, the perceived existence of a fashion or common signaling system can do so. A custom is a *consequence* of independently motivated actions that happen to be similar to each other, whereas a common signaling system *causes* action via the joint force of expectations and a desire to coordinate with other users of the system. The existence of an established fashion *causes* an action that is consistent with it via the presence of expectations and the desire to imitate the trendy. Depending on the context, one might copy those in proximity, those in similar situations, those with similar characteristics, or those who are similar in some other relevant way. One may copy either what one perceives to be the most frequent action or the most successful actors. Women buy very high heels not for the (zero) comfort of the shoe, but instead because they want to be fashionable, copy trendsetters, and expect other women in their circle to do the same. Once a fashion is established, it will induce actions in line with it. I thus define a descriptive norm as follows (Bicchieri 2006):

> *A descriptive norm is a pattern of behavior such that individuals prefer to conform to it on condition that they believe that most people in their reference network conform to it* (empirical expectation).

There are two elements here that differentiate a descriptive norm from a shared custom. In the case of a descriptive norm, people do not prefer to engage in a particular behavior irrespective of what others do. Instead, their preference for conformity is *conditional* upon observing (or believing) how others act. The "others" in this case must be somehow relevant to the actor. The *reference network* may be scattered, and may not necessarily coincide with groups one associates with daily. In the television series *The Sopranos*, many of the characters' behaviors were based on what they (wrongly) believed to be the customary ways in Italy, only to realize later on that modern Italians had moved well beyond those patterns. A young woman in Philadelphia wearing very high heels will probably not care what other women do in India, or even New Orleans. Her reference network may be the "fashionable" crowd in her town, those who she is likely to meet and give her a chance to "show off," or it may be a celebrity, magazine starlets, or TV series that girls in her reference network follow.[7] In the case of significant media influence, it is important to recognize that those who watch the television

---

7.  The TV show *Sex and the City* was associated with a spike in sales of Manolo Blahnik shoes.

program or read the popular magazine know that "everyone is reading/watching that" where "everyone" presumably refers to people that matter to one's choice to adopt a fashion. One of the reasons the media can be so influential in initiating or changing behavior is precisely the viewer or reader's awareness that many others in her reference network receive the same message.

In descriptive norms, expectations about what others are doing play a decisive role in choosing (or avoiding) an action, as in their absence different actions may be chosen. The main difference between a custom and a descriptive norm lies in the *reasons* why people follow them, since from an observational viewpoint, the practices may look identical. Understanding this distinction is crucial if we want to promote behavioral change. To change a negative custom, we may want to start by trying to convince individuals that a particular action or practice—though it meets a need—has serious drawbacks, and then propose feasible alternatives. People normally have factual beliefs about the consequences of their actions, and changing those beliefs is the first step to changing behavior. With descriptive norms, we have to engage the norm-following group in a more complex way, as expectations play a crucial role in sustaining the practice. To enact change, the empirical expectations of most participants have to change. This proves to be challenging, as change, to succeed, has to be synchronized. If I wear very high heels because of the drive to imitate the fashionable and the concurring belief that most women in my social network now wear them, it is not sufficient to observe a few women behaving differently (especially if they are not trendsetters).[8] I must be convinced that very high heels

8. Trendsetters are early adopters, people who start (or follow early on) a new trend before most other people. Psychologists still debate whether there are specific character traits that make people trendsetters, apart from their social position (some may be in positions of power or privilege). I discuss trendsetters' characteristics in much more detail in chapter 5.

are now out of fashion. The same goes for a signaling system. Since our goal is coordinated communication, we have to be convinced that everybody we may communicate with is moving to another system of signals before we change, too. Coordinated change is obviously critical. How this can be accomplished is the subject of the last two chapters, where I discuss social change. What should be clear is that the means employed to change a collective practice must be tailored to its nature.

## Imitation and Coordination

Why people have conditional preferences, why they prefer to do something if they expect others to do it, and why some behaviors become viral are all questions relevant to understanding social change, especially change that involves abandoning or creating norms. Economic, legal, and political changes often instigate or accompany norm change. Yet if norms, descriptive or otherwise, exist because followers have certain preferences and expectations, exogenous changes might not be sufficient to induce meaningful behavioral change. In any event, they will be successful only if they produce and coordinate a collective change in expectations.

In his essay "On Sumptuary Laws," Montaigne ([1580] 2003) cleverly observed that sixteenth-century French laws aiming at restricting superfluous and excessive consumption among the merchant class often had the opposite effect.

> The way by which our laws attempt to regulate idle and vain expenses in meat and clothes, seems to be quite contrary to the end designed. . . : For to enact that none but princes shall eat turbot, shall wear velvet or gold lace, and interdict these things to the people, what is it but to bring them into a greater esteem, and to set every one more agog to eat and wear them? (Montaigne [1580] 2003, 300)

In this case, prohibiting imitation of the aristocratic ways made them ever' more attractive to commoners. If anything, preferences were reinforced.

In other cases exogenous triggers may work quite well. When we want to coordinate with others, any change in expectations will lead to a change in (conditional) preferences and behavior. An external intervention that credibly changes social expectations will most certainly produce a change in preferences in this setting. On September 3, 1967, traffic in Sweden switched from driving on the left-hand side of the road to the right. The change was mandated by the government and went on smoothly, presumably because nobody wanted to keep driving on the left side of the road when the expectation was that now everybody would drive on the right-hand side.

Coordination is different from imitation. With imitation, those I imitate do not expect me to behave like they do and may not even know they are being imitated, so my expectations are unilateral. When a girl imitates an actress or the fashionable group in her school, they do not expect *her* to act as they do. What matters is that she expects *them* to act in a certain way. And this is true for each and every imitator. With coordination, expectations are instead multilateral. If you and I want to coordinate on wearing a bandanna of the same color, it matters what each of us expects the other to do. To succeed, our expectations have to match. An external intervention can potentially change social behavior if it works as a coordinating device, changing multilateral expectations. It is much less apt to succeed with imitation, unless it mandates a change in the imitated party.

Many descriptive norms do not directly fulfill a coordination function, even if we observe what appears to be coordinated behavior. It is often noticed that portfolio managers tend to make similar financial choices and offer similar advice to clients. One reason for this is that nobody is capable of predicting market gyrations, and in case the market tanks it is better to be aligned with the herd, so as to diffuse responsibility for a bad choice and relativize losses. Those managers do not intentionally coordinate, but rather imitate each other. Imitative behavior is widespread in every society. When uncertain, we look at what others are doing to resolve insecurity about making a decision. Before buying a refrigerator or a car, or hiring a landscaper, we often go to websites that list buyers' comments about products and services. Websites like Angie's List, Yahoo, or Amazon owe their fortune to social proof, our tendency to imitate others' choices because we grant them superior knowledge of the product or service (they bought it!).

Imitation, or conformity to others' behavior, has two components: *informational* and *normative* (Deutsch and Gerard 1955). In new, uncertain, or ambiguous situations, we often turn to others to gather information and obtain guidance. Imitation may be rational if collecting information is very hard or very costly, if we lack expertise, or instead if the choice is unimportant, so a wrong decision is not the end of the world. When many people make similar choices, we tend to take it as evidence of effective, adaptive behavior. Note that large numbers are not necessary to induce imitation. People often imitate the behavior of the successful, guessing that some observable traits correlate with their accomplishments. "Dress for success" is a glaring example of this naïve belief.

We all have a natural desire "to be correct," and often what is correct is defined by our social reality: I know I am a good runner when I compare my record to those of other runners. The case of financial managers is a little different: their herding behavior has the effect of minimizing potential losses. In situations of great uncertainty, it pays to "follow the herd," for if circumstances deteriorate, one will not look that bad (*"everyone was doing it!"*).

Besides being correct, people also want to be liked, to belong, and to "go along with the crowd." We often adopt the prevailing group standards and behaviors to gain (or avoid losing) social appreciation, respect, and acceptance. In the case of informational influence, there is no social pressure to conform to other people's views and beliefs, nor is one expected to conform. As I said, expectations are unilateral. With normative influence, there may or may not be group pressure to conform. That is, one may conform because one wants to gain acceptance or be liked, but a lack of conformity will not necessarily be reproached by the group.

Let us go back for a moment to our fashion slave. What motivates her to buy those uncomfortable, high-heel shoes? Both informational and normative influences are likely at work. On the one hand, she wants to imitate the fashionable crowd, as looking at what they wear is giving her valuable information about what is now "in." On the other hand, being fashionable makes her feel she belongs to a valuable group, and she will possibly become more popular if she dresses like them. However, nobody is going to require that she wears high heels, and nobody will spend time and energy reprimanding her for not doing so.

A similar case was reported by a participant in the Penn-UNICEF training course on social norms. The wife of a village chief independently decided to breastfeed her children from birth. This was unusual behavior because it was widely believed that colostrum was dirty and might damage the baby. The fact that the woman was powerful and that her children seemed healthy "despite" being breastfed at an early age induced a wave of imitation. In this case, there was the normative influence of wanting to imitate and please the powerful in addition to the informational influence of the confidence that she displayed when defying old habits.

A different case is one in which employees in a coffee shop "salt" the tip jar. Here they play on the common tendency of "doing as others do" and wish clients will be induced to leave a tip, like others appear to have done. They hope clients will feel social pressure to leave a tip. Again, there is no evident reproach for not doing it, aside from perhaps a slight embarrassment on the client's part. Fashions and fads, "imitating the successful," social proof, and salting the tip jar are all examples of behaviors that are driven by unilateral expectations.

Now think of coordinating on a signal, a multilateral situation. Signals may be as complex as a language, or as simple as traffic lights. Here the normative influence may vary from nil to significant. If I stop using a signal that many others use, as in the case of a widely spoken language, nobody will possibly care, and I will be the only one to pay a price, for I will be ignored. But think of stopping (unilaterally) to obey traffic lights. Running a red light not only endangers my own life, but also endangers other people's lives as well. To safely use traffic lights, everyone must expect that all drivers stop at red and go at green. If people start disregarding the signal, coordination is lost, and everybody is put at risk. When we call those who disregard a red light "crazy" or "idiots," we imply that they are doing something that can damage them too. So, there certainly is a normative influence here, but is it superseding everything else? What are the *main* reasons why people stop at a red light? Is there a temptation not to? If there were no blame for disregarding traffic signals, would people disregard them? If your reason to stop is that you expect other drivers to obey traffic lights and thus drive smoothly and safely, your empirical expectation and the desire to coordinate with other drivers are what matters most to your choice. Traffic conventions, once established, do not require the force of law or social enforcement to sustain themselves. It is in everyone's self-interest to follow the convention, as deviation does not pay.

The coordination motive is very different from imitation, in that expectations are multilateral and stem from a desire to harmonize our actions with those of others so that each of our individual goals can be achieved. Signaling systems, language rules, rules of etiquette, and dress codes are all examples of descriptive norms that are driven by multilateral expectations.

A preference for following a descriptive norm may involve both informational and normative influences, or the wish to coordinate with others, but *this preference remains conditional on empirical expectations alone.* This means that if these expectations were to change, preferences and behavior would change too. There is a causal relationship between expectations, preferences, and behavior. If we want to claim that descriptive norms have causal influence, it is not sufficient to look for a correlation between expectations and behavior as evidence (i.e., to observe that certain expectations and certain behaviors frequently occur together). There are many correlations that are causally irrelevant. Wearing warm clothes in winter is a collective habit motivated by the need to keep the body warm. We do not choose to wear warm clothes *because* we expect others to wear them.[9] Our choice is independent of expectations. If we were to query Philadelphia residents, we would find out that everyone expects other residents to wear warm clothes in winter. And we may also observe that the individuals we have queried wear warm clothes in winter. We do have a correlation between expectations and choices (they occur together in a consistent way). But are those expectations *causally relevant* to the behavior we observe? Or does the observed behavior instead generate the expectation?

Causal relations involve counterfactual dependence: A and B both occurred, but if A had not occurred (and B had no other sufficient cause), B would not have occurred either. For example, if we think that lack of water is the main reason why people do not build latrines, we must be prepared to say that, if water

---

9. That said, the *kind* of warm clothes we wear may be fashion-based, and thus influenced by expectations.

were abundant (contrary to the fact that it is scarce), then latrines would be built and used.[10] I am greatly simplifying here, but these are the basic ideas. We can be pretty sure that were we to observe people going around scantily dressed in a harsh winter, our expectations would change, but our behavior would not. When I was teaching at Carnegie Mellon University, many computer students braved the winter snow in T-shirts, shorts, and flip-flops. Most of us looked at them as alien nerds as we snuggled in our warm coats.

My view about descriptive norms, as opposed to customs, is that they have a causal influence on behavior. Expecting members of our reference network to behave according to the descriptive norm (i.e., expecting a consistent pattern of behavior), and having preferences conditional on these expectations induces individuals to conform to that pattern. In this case, we would observe that expectations and behavior are strongly correlated, but to know why we must know what mechanism produces the correlation. To find out, we need to experimentally manipulate one or more factors (the independent variables) to observe their effect on behavior (the dependent variable). It is important to give both independent and dependent variables precise operational definitions that specify how to manipulate the independent variable (in our case, empirical expectations) and how to measure the dependent variable (conforming behavior).

In the next chapter I will discuss at length how to measure norms, and in particular, how to manipulate expectations to assess causality. For example, one way to influence empirical expectations is to tell one group of participants in an experiment

10. Many interventions have been based on the belief that economic or ecological conditions are the most important causal factors, and that changing them would dramatically improve the situation. Since many such interventions failed, we must be aware that it is of foremost importance to correctly identify causal factors.

about the behavior of other participants in a similar past experiment (thereby changing their empirical expectations). Another group of participants (the control group) instead is not given any information. If there is a significant difference in behavior between the two groups, we can be fairly certain that expectations matter to choice (Bicchieri and Xiao 2009).

Another, less precise way to check for a causal connection is to ask counterfactual or simply hypothetical questions. If a behavioral pattern is very common, we may ask those who conform to it what they would do if most people in their reference network were to behave differently. Would they stick to the behavior? If not, why not?

Empirical expectations must be coupled with a conditional preference for conforming; otherwise they will have no influence on behavior. Conformity may be driven by the desire to imitate or to coordinate with others. But what about when normative influences play a stronger role? What about behaviors that are keenly endorsed by a reference network, so much so that deviation gets punished and compliance praised? What about situations in which the expectation of approval and disapproval, the acknowledged presence of sanctions, act as important motivators? In these cases, we are dealing with social norms.

## SOCIAL NORMS

Consider the following scene. A long line of people is waiting to buy a ticket for a popular movie. Someone approaches the first person in line and offers a few dollars to take her place. When I give this example to my class, students react with outrage. "If I were in line behind the guy, I would get mad," and "it is unfair to those who wait patiently" are common reactions. If the payment is to literally cut in front of the first person, then the exchange is imposing a negative externality on everyone behind her in the queue because they now have to wait one person longer. She has no right to sell her place. Indeed, paying for jumping a queue elicits strong disapproval.[11]

Alternatively, think what would happen if somebody at the end of a long line went to the person who was first in line, and offered him money to switch places. In this case, nobody would be disadvantaged. Nevertheless, many would find this exchange objectionable. A common concern is that if we allow people to jump ahead in queues of all sorts (as opposed to waiting in line), there is a fundamental sense that people are not treated equally. If economic efficiency is the argument, why not allow someone to sell her vote as well? While inefficient, queues embody a standard of fairness in which nobody is more important than another and anyone can be subject to a wait. In a world where people can buy their way up, we can imagine a class of people who are rich and never have to wait, and a class who always must wait because their time is less valuable as determined by what they can pay. Many would find such a world repulsive.

In the first example, people would feel entitled to protest, even block the transaction. In the second, even if we deeply dislike the deal, we usually feel we do not have a right to complain. Why this difference? What makes us feel we have a right to expect certain behaviors but not others? The second transaction is a *private* one, and though we may dislike it, we recognize that people have a right to conduct their private business as they like. The first example instead created a *public* negative externality, as everybody in the line has to wait longer. In

---

11. Stanley Milgram (1992) conducted an experiment by sending his students around with the instructions to cut in lines at ticket counters. In more than half of the cases, people reacted very negatively. Reactions ranged from dirty looks, to verbal protests, all the way to physical shoves.

this case there would likely be much social support for openly and loudly complaining, as opposed to the second case. When actions create public negative externalities, societies develop rules to curb these effects. Examples are rules that enforce cooperation or reciprocation, which are necessary to support social interactions. Without cooperation and trust, it becomes exceedingly hard, if not impossible, to sustain social exchanges. Yet there are other social rules (in addition to pro-social ones) that can elicit collective support. Child marriage does not seem to curb any particular, public negative externality. In a society where child marriage is the norm, waiting to marry off one's daughter will only produce negative consequences for the family and the unmarried girl, not the broader society. Yet witnesses to a contravention in such a society will feel entitled to blame, gossip about, ostracize, or pity the girl. The socially imposed *ought* is present in these practices, even if it is not borne out of a pro-social necessity.

I believe that the difference between rules that enforce pro-sociality and other sorts of shared practices stems from their origins. The latter may have evolved from simpler descriptive norms that, with time, acquired a special symbolic meaning (as I discuss further in chapter 3), whereas the former directly evolved from a collective need to guarantee a measure of social order. Once they are established, both kinds of rules ultimately share the same features that identify them as social norms.

Social norms perform a double function. They tell us that particular behavioral responses are warranted in situations that are sufficiently similar to each other: you do not cut in a line of cars waiting at an intersection, and similarly you do not jump in front of people queuing for a cab or waiting to be served in a pastry shop. Social norms also express social approval or disapproval of such behaviors—they tell us how we *ought* to act. Social norms are often called *injunctive norms*: what we collectively believe ought to be done, what is socially approved or disapproved of (Rivis and Sheeran 2003). As in the case of descriptive norms, there are ambiguities in this definition, which may confound shared moral norms with social norms. For example, the moral codes a society or group shares prescribe and/or proscribe specific behaviors, entail evaluations and judgments, and signal the mutual expectation that we ought to abide by them. Though some may argue that there really is no difference between social and moral norms, others would object.

My objective here is not to examine the nature of morality. All I want to call attention to is that there is an element of (social) unconditionality to what we take to be moral rules that is not present in social norms, in the sense that one's personal moral convictions are the primary motivator of one's actions, and such convictions overwhelm any social considerations. I am agnostic as to the existence of moral norms above and beyond the reasons people have to follow them. What I want to say is that—when we obey what we take to be a "moral" rule— we do not condition our choice on the behaviors and beliefs of other people, at least in principle. So fairness may be a social norm for some, but a deeply held moral norm for others. There is nothing about fairness that makes it moral, apart from one's view that it is a value that one should pursue as best as one can, even if one witnesses unfair behavior all the time.

From a purely descriptive standpoint, what we call "morality" is a code of conduct that guides behavior. Moral codes regulate the behaviors that a society considers to be most important, including behaviors that directly or indirectly affect others: rules against killing, causing pain, and deceiving are all examples of rules that prohibit causing direct or indirect harm.[12] Moral codes, however, differ among cultures, as they may also include rules of purity, honor, or loyalty that could conflict with what we

---

12. These rules are often subject to exceptions. We might believe that we must not harm our friends, but it is acceptable to harm our foes.

take to be "do no harm" injunctions. Honor killing may be seen, by those that stand by it, as a moral duty. In this case, values of honor and purity supersede rules against killing. In fact, some cultures believe that the actions of a "stray woman" bring shame to her entire family, and this shame must be washed away with her blood (Feldner 2000). What matters here is that every society tends to "moralize" certain behaviors. This process of moralization happens at an individual level too, but is not uniform in its spread. When we say that a norm has been internalized, we often refer to the development of moral beliefs that correspond to societal standards. These beliefs become an independent motivation to conform, as deviations are often accompanied by guilt.

A norm that dictates female genital cutting (FGC) may embed important ideals of purity and honor, among others, and be part of the moral code of a group or society. For some individuals, this rule may be so important that it becomes (socially) unconditional. These individuals do not need to take into consideration the behavior of their peers when deciding whether to follow the rule. For other individuals, the choice to abide by the rule may be conditional on their social expectations. This is why I do not want to talk of moral rules in general, as if they had a status independent of the reasons of the individuals who follow them. Honor killing may be a social norm for some, a moral norm for others. All of that said, I can think of situations in which an individual who has moralized a rule may fail to follow it (and not because of weakness of will). Also moral rules can be conditional, but not in the same sense social norms are. Some moral rules are more important than others and take precedence in cases of conflict, and in some situations it is acceptable to abandon or adapt some rules. In a state of anarchy, one may conclude that harming and deceiving is the only way to survive, but one may do so with great anguish and guilt and still endorse (if not follow) general rules against harming and deceiving (Bicchieri 2006).

I mention here the strong emotion of guilt because it is often associated, as a moral emotion, with our commitment and conformity to what we take to be moral rules. Yet, as I have noted elsewhere (Bicchieri 2010), emotions are not a necessary hallmark of morality. One may feel guilty at openly choosing an unfair division of money, keeping more for oneself, but conveniently give nothing to an unaware party, provided it is plain that one's unfair choice is hidden (Dana, Weber, and Kuang 2007). Would we be willing to say that fairness matters when one is "watched," but that it loses its appeal when one can cheat in secret? It seems that a better way to distinguish, as far as we want to make such a distinction, between the moral and the social valence of the rule is to think of the ways in which we can justify its transgression. If I am willing to defend my unfair decision by pointing out that "others are unfair too," or that "I am not really expected to act fairly on this occasion," or even that "the other party will believe his misfortune was just bad luck," it seems clear that my choice was conditional on having certain social expectations. Fairness, in these examples, is not a moral norm to be followed no matter what.

The important point to be made is that we have (in principle) reasons for upholding what we take to be moral norms that go beyond the fact that we *perceive* them to be generally upheld *by a reference network* that may reproach deviance. Our commitment to these moral norms is independent of what we expect others to believe, do, or approve/disapprove of. Social norms instead are always (socially) *conditional*, in the sense that our preference for obeying them depends upon our expectations of collective compliance. This does not mean that we may not find good reasons to support some of those norms. There are many social norms that we may find socially beneficial, like rules of fairness or reciprocity, but I maintain that most people follow them because they know that they are generally followed and because they expect most individuals in their reference network to keep following them. They also have reason to think most individuals in their reference network believe that they ought to be fair and to reciprocate in the appropriate conditions. In the absence of these social expectations, one may not reciprocate any longer, despite still believing that, in a well-functioning society, reciprocity should be the rule.

Like descriptive norms, social norms rely upon empirical expectations, that is, the belief that others in our reference network follow the norm. However, with social norms, the normative influence is strong and plays a crucial role in driving compliance. It matters to us that most people in our reference network believe we ought to conform to a certain behavioral pattern. This point must be emphasized. First, let me point out that people may think one ought to behave in a specific way for many different reasons. Parents who marry off their young daughters believe they are protecting them while simultaneously affording a good husband at a reasonable dowry price. Many Islamic countries require women to cover their bodies and faces, for reasons of modesty and family honor. Southern whites thought blacks should take menial jobs, to stress their alleged cultural and economic inferiority and ultimately to support a system that favored whites. A gang requires its members to wear particular clothes and colors to signal their group identity and show pride in belonging to that group. We think that trust should be reciprocated, because otherwise we would end up in a society in which very few transactions would occur. *For every social norm we may think of, we will find some reason why followers think it should be upheld.* When a norm is in place, we may or may not embrace what we believe are the reasons why the norm exists. In other words, we may be more or less *sensitive* or sympathetic to the norm's content.[13] Yet the social

13. I shall extensively discuss the role played by norm sensitivity in chapter 5, when I discuss norm change.

pressure to conform, expressed in the social expectation that one ought to conform, is a powerful motivator. I thus define a social norm as follows (Bicchieri 2006):[14]

> *A social norm is a rule of behavior such that individuals prefer to conform to it on condition that they believe that (a) most people in their reference network conform to it* (empirical expectation), *and (b) that most people in their reference network believe they ought to conform to it* (normative expectation).

If others believe one *ought to* conform, the reaction to non-conformity may range from slight displeasure to active or even extreme punishment.[15] It should be clear that the *ought* is not prudential, because disregarding a prudential *ought* would not normally elicit a negative sanction. My friends may think that I *ought* to diet because being obese threatens my health in many ways. However, none of them would dream of punishing me because of my bad eating habits; they might tell me that I ought to stop, but this would be said out of concern for my wellbeing rather than wanting to put me "back in line."

14. I do not use "behavioral pattern" but instead talk of behavioral rules, for the reason that often norms proscribe behaviors, so we do not typically observe the behavior proscribed by the rule. It is also the case that a norm may exist but not be followed at a given time if the potential followers' expectations are not met (Bicchieri 2006, 11).

15. It is important to clarify that this imposed *ought* is normative in a strong sense, and not necessarily prudential. Other models, such as the theory of planned behavior (and its predecessor, the reasoned action approach; see Ajzen, Albarracín, and Hornik 2007; Fishbein and Ajzen 2011), do not make this distinction, and failing to do so can be problematic. The theory of planned behavior relies on the measurement of behavior-specific attitudes, "subjective norms," and perceived behavioral control to collectively predict behavioral intentions. The subjective norms in the model refer to individuals' expectations of the degree to which "important others" would approve or disapprove of their performing a given behavior (Ajzen 1991, 195).

The extent of the social reaction to a norm transgression varies, depending on how important or central to social life a norm is, how entrenched it is, and what sort of real or perceived harm disobedience creates. It is also important to acknowledge that many norms admit of variations in behavior and that the acceptable range of behaviors may be substantial, thus increasing uncertainty as to the scope of deviations and, consequently, the appropriate severity of sanctions.

It is often the case that norms are not "all or nothing" affairs. Fair divisions, for example, may include a 60–40 percent share as acceptable. Norms of decorum may tolerate slight variations in unkemptness (though up to a point). This quality of degrees of acceptability for a norm is well-addressed in the Return Potential Model (Jackson 1965). The Return Potential Model is a method of visualizing acceptable behavior as constrained by norms: on a Y-axis one would plot the amount of approval one could garner by engaging in an action, and on an X-axis one would plot the intensity or amount of a behavior being engaged in (see the example reproduced in Figure 1.1).

Despite having some predictive efficacy, the model's normative component falls short: First, the model always includes a normative predictor, regardless of whether or not the behavior being predicted is normative in nature. Second, the model does not take descriptive norms into account (a limitation acknowledged by one of the theory's founders; see Fishbein 2007). Finally, as mentioned earlier, the model does not appear to differentiate between second-order prudential expectations and second-order expectations of a stronger normative nature (Ajzen 1991). In other words, the model's normative measurements are too broad: when taking the approach of the theory of planned behavior, it will be impossible to determine whether a respondent believes that her peers believe that engaging in a particular behavior is wrong because it is unwise (i.e., wrong on a prudential level) or that it is wrong because it violates some shared rule (e.g., fairness). What I call normative expectations, rather than prudential ones, exert a greater influence on a decision maker when choosing whether to conform to a social norm.

For example, an individual with ten dollars in his pocket who is deciding how much money to give to a beggar might think that his friends (his reference network) will think he is selfish if he gives fewer than four dollars, but they will think that a gift of more than seven dollars is just foolish. Here, the individual assumes that there is a happy medium of donating between four and seven dollars that will garner approval from his friends.

In the plot one can identify a "point of maximum return," at which an individual will get the maximum possible approval out of an action. In the above graph, this point would be at 6 (or six dollars in the aforementioned example). The Return Potential Model assumes that norm-relevant actions can always either improve or damage one's reputation, which might not necessarily be the case (e.g., refusing to defecate in the open when in a

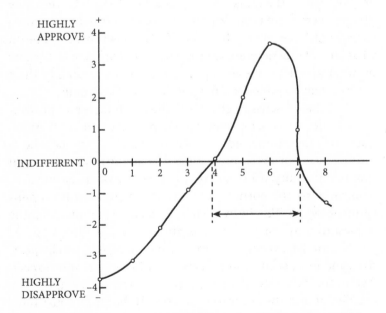

FIGURE 1.1 The Return Potential Model (reproduced from Jackson 1965).

Western society would not be likely to improve one's reputation, but engaging in it would certainly damage one's reputation).

Additionally, there is also a range of behaviors that are seen as acceptable: in the earlier example, a gift of between four and seven dollars was perceived to be acceptable. In Bangladesh, a father might think that marrying off his daughter below the age of seven is too young (she is just a child!) but marrying her off after the age of fifteen is too old (people might think she is having premarital sex if she gets any older). Similarly, each behavior can garner a range of approval or disapproval. That is, the height of the Y-axis demonstrates the intensity of positive and negative sanctions that norm-adherence or norm-violations incur. The Return Potential Model can also reveal how much agreement (i.e., crystallization) there is about a norm (though this is not shown in Figure 1.1): there might be disagreement about how important the norm is or about where the range of acceptable behaviors lies. The more disagreement there is on the importance of a norm or on what is considered "acceptable," the more disagreement there will be on what kind of sanctions are appropriate. The more people disagree on what sanctions are appropriate, the more uncertainty there will be about the sanctions' magnitudes and likelihoods.

As I shall discuss in chapter 5, the combination of punishment (mild, serious, or absent) and a person's sensitivity to the norm will determine individual compliance. Someone who is indifferent to or even disagrees with the norm's content will avoid conformity if no sanction is present, whereas someone who supports the norm will tend to conform even if no punishment looms. This individual will usually recognize that the request to conform is legitimate, and respond positively.

Normative expectations may also be accompanied by positive sanctions, such as liking, appreciation, trust, and respect. Again, the existence of strong positive rewards may move the indifferent and the contrarian to comply, but it will just reinforce the supporter's conviction. This is why norms that are (or are believed to be) onerous to follow are usually accompanied by strong negative and positive sanctions: in a society in which cooperation or reciprocation with strangers is perceived to be difficult to obtain, an honest cooperator is praised, and a non-reciprocator will acquire a bad reputation. A culture that holds ideals of family respectability and honor, along with the beliefs that women are men's property, are weak, and are easily seduced, will impose strict rules of conduct on women and punish transgressions harshly. Honor killing is an extreme measure, but the reward is high status and social respect. Sometimes even norms that are not particularly onerous to follow, like a gang's dress code or other outward signs of belonging, are supported by significant sanctions, in that disregarding them defies the group's identity and signals disrespect. In the TV show *Sons of Anarchy*, a man who belongs to a motorcycle club is a "badass." Yet, "You know you're a badass when you'll strap down an ex-member and set his back on fire to remove his club tattoo."[16] Small, close-knit groups are particularly defensive about the norms that identify them, and are ready to punish deviators who threaten the very identity of the group.

Let me point out again that the cost of deviating from a descriptive norm, especially a convention, is very different from the cost of deviating from a social norm. Deviating from a convention, such as a linguistic one, is inherently costly to the deviating party. Once a convention is established, everyone does better by following it, especially when it is expected that everyone else adheres to it. Norms are not self-enforcing in the sense that conventions are. With a norm, there is often the temptation to transgress it—this is precisely why norms must be socially enforced. Without these systems of sanctions, the norm could easily fall apart.

16. In the show, the person had been required to remove his tattoo, and since he did not, they burned it off of him so no one would mistake him for a member in good standing. http://www.sidereel.com/posts/36137-news-missing-sons-of-anarchy-top-10-badass-moments-featured.

Here, my aim is not to draw a taxonomy of norms and accompanying sanctions, but rather to stress the relation of conditional preferences to empirical and normative expectations. I have argued that conformity to a social norm can be completely independent of attributing value to the norm one obeys. We may be induced to obey norms we dislike, or reject behaviors that we find perfectly appropriate. Often, however, especially with norms that are well established, norm followers tend to *value* what the norm stands for. An external observer may be induced to think that, since people have a positive attitude toward a norm, they may obey it *regardless* of what others around them do. Social expectations do not seem important anymore!

In fact, we may be tempted to explain why a given behavior persists by referring to the observation that most individuals in the network where it is commonly practiced share the conviction that it is good and valuable. We do not seem to be facing conditional preferences here: individuals behave in a similar way because they all think such behavior carries some advantage. Is this a correct conclusion? Recall what I said about causality. It involves counterfactual dependence: all other things being equal, if an individual did not have a positive belief toward $x$, she would not do $x$. What seems required is changing the positive belief alone. Information interventions failed at changing some negative practices, such as new mothers' refusal to breastfeed immediately after giving birth, because they missed the fact that people had social expectations and conditional preferences based on them. Information was introduced with the intention of changing factual and personal normative beliefs about the importance of immediate and continuous breastfeeding, the damages of giving newborns water (often contaminated), and the connection between infant mortality and traditional practices. Such interventions were not accompanied by the understanding that the practice was supported by widely held social expectations, both empirical and normative. Even if we were to succeed at convincing a young mother of the benefits of immediate breastfeeding, would she dare incur the wrath of her mother-in-law, the scorn of other women, and the accusation that she was risking the life of her child? This problem is particularly acute in cases of *pluralistic ignorance* (a concept that I will explore later on).

I realize that it might be a bit daunting to keep track of the various factors that determine the nature of a collective behavior. Now that I have clarified the features of each collective practice (in terms of preferences and social expectations), I have included a visual summary of the diagnostic process of identifying a social norm and differentiating it from other collective behaviors in Figure 1.2. I will explore in the following chapter how we can reach a diagnostic conclusion through measurement.

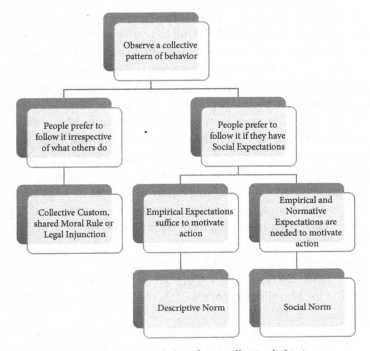

FIGURE 1.2 Diagnostic process of identifying collective behaviors. Source: C. Bicchieri, *Social Norms, Social Change*. Penn-UNICEF Lecture, July 2012.

## BELIEF TRAPS: PLURALISTIC IGNORANCE

Consider the case of a social norm N present in a network G. We know the following:

1. All members of G believe that all other members of G follow N.
2. All members of G believe that all other members of G believe one ought to follow N.

However, it is not true that all members of G believe one ought to follow N. In fact, the majority of individuals dislike N and do not think one ought to follow it. In a UNICEF study about violence on children, it was stunning to realize that caregivers who report a negative judgment on punishment still punish in large numbers (country median: 50 percent).[17] One possible explanation for this disparity is that these caregivers observe corporal punishment, or corporal punishment's consequences, such as bruises, and have no reason to believe that those who conform to the norm dislike it as much as they do. They dare not speak out or openly transgress, for fear of being regarded as weak or uncaring parents. In this way a norm nobody actually likes will survive, and if deviations occur, they will be kept secret. This is an example of *pluralistic ignorance*, a cognitive state in which each member of a group believes her personal normative beliefs and preferences are different from those of similarly situated others, even if public behavior is identical (Miller and McFarland 1987). The following set of conditions is a fertile ground for pluralistic ignorance (Bicchieri 2006, ch. 5; 2014):

a) Individuals engage in social comparison with their reference network. We constantly observe what others

17. www.childinfo.org./discipline.html.

do, and from these observations we get clues about appropriate behavior, others' preferences, beliefs, and so forth. In the case of norms, we are influenced by the behavior of other network members, but we do not know the true distribution of their beliefs and preferences, which we try to infer from observing their behavior.

b) Others' behavior is observable. If not, then the consequences of such behavior are observable.[18]

c) No transparent communication is possible. Because of shared values, religious reasons, or simply the fear of being shunned or ridiculed as a deviant or just different, we do not express views that we think will put us at a disadvantage.

d) We assume that, unlike us, others' behavior is consistent with their preferences and beliefs. There are several possible reasons why this might occur. Fear of embarrassment or the desire to fit in are not easy to observe in others, so we may come to believe that we experience these emotions more strongly than others do. Another possible cause of the self/other discrepancy is the *fundamental attribution error* (Ross 1977): we tend to overestimate the extent to which others act on private motives (beliefs, preferences), while we instead attribute our own behavior to external factors (social pressure in this case).

e) We infer that all but us endorse the observed norm. We discount personal evidence in favor of what we observe and take it at face value.

---

18. For example, compliance with norms that regulate sexual behavior or other unobservable behaviors can be assessed by observing the presence or absence of the consequences of such behaviors. In the case of norms that prohibit pre-marital sex, teen pregnancies would be a sign that the norm has been flouted.

All end up conforming to the public norm, oblivious to the possibility that they are participants in a group dynamic in which all pretend to support the norm, while in fact all dislike it.

In a state of pluralistic ignorance, individuals are caught in a belief trap and will keep following a norm that they deeply dislike. How long can this last? One may suspect that a norm that is so disliked would not be stable, since even small shocks to the system of beliefs that support it would lead to its demise. Once the frequency of true beliefs is conveyed to the relevant population, a change would occur. Such change may be feasible with a descriptive norm, but it is much more difficult to obtain in the case of a social norm.

Berkowitz and Perkins (1987; see also Berkowitz 2005) have taken advantage of the effectiveness of *beliefs shocks*, public revelations of pluralistic ignorance, when attempting to change maladaptive descriptive norms that are maintained by pluralistic ignorance, particularly alcohol consumption on college campuses. Their approach is designed to stop people from engaging in a collective practice by informing them that participation rates (typically drinking rates) are lower than they might appear. Such information serves to update a target audience's empirical expectations. This approach, when properly implemented, is effective at combatting descriptive norms that suffer from pluralistic ignorance (which are supported by inaccurate empirical expectations), but is not effective at changing independent practices, such as customs (if you inform people that fewer of their peers use umbrellas than they previously thought, why should they care?), or social norms, which are additionally supported by normative expectations.

Since a social norm is supported by normative expectations, it is not sufficient to publically disclose that most individuals dislike the norm and would like to do something different. The participants must also be sure that its abandonment will not be followed by negative sanctions. People face a double credibility problem here: they must believe that the information they receive about others' true beliefs is accurate, and they must also believe that everyone else is committed to change their ways. There are many ways to achieve these goals, and there are several examples in the literature of successful changes of negative norms by means of information campaigns, public declarations, and common pledges (Bicchieri and Mercier 2014). Any successful change, as I shall argue in the last two chapters, must change both empirical and normative expectations, their relative order depending on whether a norm is being created or abandoned.

Whether we are facing pluralistic ignorance is an entirely empirical question. A few years ago, a friend from UNICEF presented me with the following data, confessing she was at a loss as to how to interpret them.[19]

She noted that in Sudan, Djibuti, and Burkina Faso there was a significant discrepancy between the prevalence of FGC and its support among women who would have been directly involved in getting their daughters cut. However, in places like Chad, prevalence and support were very much in line.[20] At the time, I knew that women were only questioned about their attitudes, not about their expectations,

19. The data sources in Table 1.3 are UNICEF global databases, based on DHS, MICS, and other nationally representative surveys. See more at: http://data.unicef.org/child-protection/fgmc.html#sthash.jV8FtLDS.dpuf.
20. It is important to notice that the 49.4 percent of women who supported the practice in Chad might not overlap with the 44.9 percent who actually engaged in the practice. In this respect, it is important to consider the strength of a social norm in a population. For example, we would have to

Table 1.3

## FEMALE GENITAL CUTTING PREVALENCE VS. SUPPORT OF THE PRACTICE AMONG WOMEN 15-49

| Area name | Time period | Prevalence | Support | Dataset sources |
|---|---|---|---|---|
| Somalia | 2006 | 97.9 | 64.5 | MICS 2006 |
| Guinea | 2005 | 95.6 | 69.2 | DHS 2005 |
| Djibouti | 2006 | 93.1 | 36.6 | MICS 2006, table CP5. |
| Egypt | 2008 | 91.1 | 54 | DHS 2008, table 15.1, p. 197 |
| Sudan | 2006 | 89.3 | 23.7 | SHHS 2006 |
| Mali | 2007 | 85.2 | 76 | DHS 2006 |
| Ethiopia | 2005 | 74.3 | 31.4 | DHS 2005, table 16.13, p. 253 |
| Burkina Faso | 2006 | 72.5 | 11.1 | MICS 2006, table CP5. |
| Mauritania | 2007 | 72.2 | 53.4 | MICS 2007 |
| Chad | 2004 | 44.9 | 49.4 | DHS 2004, table 11.1, page 170 |
| Yemen | 1997 | 22.6 | 41 | DHS 1997 |

especially normative ones. It was possible that in Sudan women did not dare express their true preferences and beliefs and kept performing a ritual that was expected of them, without being aware they were not the lone deviants. It is also possible that women knew about other women's opinions, but were forced to perform the ritual, or that the practice was so ubiquitous that it had become naturalized and

consider the central tendency (that is, how strong the norm is) in different groups, as well as the norm dispersion (that is, how uniformly groups conform to the norm). Typically, a social norm is very strong where there is a clear and high central tendency and very little dispersion.

people did not even consider alternatives, even if they might not have had a strong preference for it. To know the reasons for the discrepancy, we must be able to measure normative expectations, and check whether perceived and objective consensus differ. Measuring expectations is precisely what I recommend doing in the next chapter, when I tackle the issue of norm measurement.

## CONCLUSION

Many programs designed to curb the incidence of sexual behaviors that spread AIDS, induce people to build and use latrines, educate girls, or convince families not to marry off their very young daughters have failed. Program failures have taught us that causal factors that drive collective behaviors have to be addressed in order to change descriptive and social norms, and the first, most important step in a successful intervention is precisely to identify causal relations. I have maintained that experiments are the best way to assess causal relations. However, it may be very difficult to manipulate personal evaluations in an experiment.[21] What we can do is influence expectations about what others do or believe should be done (that is, alter normative and empirical expectations). In other words, if we were to believe that social expectations play no role in directing behavior, then altering them experimentally (creating or eliminating them) should not change the behavior of individuals who have expressed a positive evaluation (through a survey) of the behavior in question. I will return to this important point in the chapter on measurement. For the time being, let me remind the reader that the link between personal normative beliefs and behavior is not necessarily strong (Eagly and Chaiken 1993). People may *say* that they approve or disapprove of something, but when we look at their actions we often see no consistency with their evaluative judgments.

In defining social norms as I did, I have stressed the role of conditional preferences and social expectations. In other words, I have relied upon the *reasons* that make people behave

21. We may give damning information about a company (it uses slave labor!) and thus change a subject's personal evaluation of that company, but it would be much harder to change personal evaluations about common, valued, and long-established practices.

as they do. Understanding these reasons is critical to instigating social change, as I shall discuss further in chapter 3. If we believe social norms have causal efficacy, we must be ready to show that, were the expectations that support a norm absent, the norm would no longer be followed. Since the preference for following a social norm is conditional upon having the right kind of social expectations, altering expectations should affect behavior in significant ways.

Again, experiments are the best means to check whether empirical and normative expectations matter to choice and under what conditions. Yet there are many situations in which experiments are difficult or impossible to perform, and we may have to fall back on surveys and vignettes to assess whether a norm is present and how and when it influences behavior. In the following chapter I shall provide tools for measuring norms and ways to check the causal pathways that link a social norm to actions.

# 2

# MEASURING NORMS

## *Consensus and Conformity*

We have seen that there are important differences between social practices. I drew a distinction between independent and interdependent behaviors, and introduced a few simple tools to help understand the nature of the behaviors we observe. Some are customs, others are descriptive norms, and others yet are social norms. Simple observation does not tell us much about the nature of such observed behavior. We need to know the reasons why people behave as they do and tease out the ones that have causal efficacy. People who follow a custom likely expect others to behave similarly, but these expectations do not influence their choice to follow their customary ways. At the opposite end of the spectrum, we have conformity to a social norm: here social expectations do matter and, provided the necessary expectations are met, conforming behavior will follow.

In this chapter, I shall focus on social norms and discuss how to determine that they both exist and have causal power. This exercise requires two sets of measures. First, we have to find out whether the pattern of behavior we observe is a social norm or is supported by one. To this effect, we need to measure the normative expectations of those engaged in the practice. If these expectations are mutually consistent, then there is widespread *consensus* that a specific behavior should be performed (or avoided). Consensus, however, does not imply conforming behavior. We may all agree that we ought to divide a good into equal parts if there is no reason to do otherwise, but if we do not expect others to proceed with an equal division, we might not feel compelled to abide by a norm of equality. Having (socially) conditional preferences means that—were social expectations absent—the norm would not be followed. The causal power of a norm depends upon the presence of the relevant social expectations and our preference to act according to them.

The second measure we should obtain assesses the conditions under which a norm will be obeyed. To obtain such a measure, we will need some manipulation of social expectations. Behavioral experiments are useful tools for this task, in that they allow us to present participants with information aimed at inducing or removing empirical and/or normative expectations. Having first established that a norm seems to apply to the situation we are concerned with, this manipulation exercise lets us determine whether individuals have conditional preferences, whether some expectations are more important than others, and how sensitive different individuals are to the norm.

The lab offers simpler, more precise, controlled tests of our hypotheses. It is easy to manipulate variables and see how behavior changes. In the field, such controlled experiments are not possible, and we need to use other tools, such as surveys and vignettes. In what follows, I will compare the two methods. In the field, we have to rely on less precise assessments, the manipulation of variables is substituted by hypothetical questions/scenarios, and unless we try to intervene, there is no chance of observing behavioral change. At most, we can say that, were expectations to change, behavior would probably change, too. I believe that controlled behavioral experiments are a useful guide to the field, in that the definition and measures of consensus and conformity can still be used in the messy world we inhabit outside the lab.

## EFFECTIVE INTERVENTIONS

In my consulting and training experience, many of the people with whom I have worked have asked me how to discriminate between customs, conventions, and social norms. When child marriage is prevalent, why do people marry off their young daughters? Do they do it because it is just a tradition that they find valuable, or do they feel compelled to do what everyone else does? If so, are there consequences for noncompliance? If decisions are interdependent, in the sense that people care about what their community does and approves of, what is the nature of this dependence? Similar questions could be raised when discussing female genital cutting (FGC), spousal or sexual violence, sexual habits, or sanitation practices. What do the groups involved think about these practices? Who are the decision-makers? Why are these practices stable? All these questions are complicated by the fact that, whereas some programs have been extraordinarily successful in eliminating damaging practices, others have failed. Was this failure related to a lack of understanding of the nature of these behaviors? Without an adequate understanding of the nature of a particular collective behavior, it is hopelessly challenging to design an effective intervention. As we saw in the first chapter, there is a difference between imitation, coordination, and acting to be approved by others. In all these cases, we care about what others do and/or believe, but the nature of the interdependence will vary, and so should the type of policy intervention.

If a practice is interdependent, in the sense that people follow it because they entertain reciprocal expectations, interventions designed to change the factual and personal normative beliefs of individuals will have little effect on actual behavior. A new mother in Sierra Leone may become convinced that feeding colostrum to the newborn is a healthy practice, that drinking water is dangerous because the local water is polluted, and that only some foods are best suited for babies. However, if her mother-in-law does not agree with these novelties, or if the elder women in the village who are the keepers of group traditions are not on board, the new mother will not be adequately motivated to change her behavior.[1] What other women in her situation do and what her mother-in-law expects her to do matter to a new mother's choice, despite all of the new information she may have about nursing, food, and healthy choices.

I called the network of people whose behavior and expectations matter to the decision maker the "reference network." The reference network is usually (but not always) quite local: people normally do not worry much about what strangers might expect of them. Sometimes the reference network includes a small group of friends and family, at other times religious leaders, and it may even comprise people who live in countries from which an individual has emigrated. Mapping the reference network is an essential part of understanding social norms and how to change them, because the norm has to change within the reference network, as I shall discuss later on.

Returning to the breastfeeding example, we know that strategies that were developed at the local level and designed to change mistaken beliefs about colostrum succeeded in changing some of the (false) factual beliefs of young mothers but did not foster new behaviors. This failure to change behavior likely stemmed from the fact that mothers-in-law and older women in general, who are regarded as the defenders of revered traditions, were not included in the intervention (Tchibindat 2012). Similar failures have plagued programs designed to encourage the adoption of preventive practices to curb the risk of HIV/AIDS. Paradoxically, it has been observed that individuals who are aware of the risks associated with HIV/AIDS and know

1. As Marie Therese Guigui of UNICEF-WCARO (UNICEF West and Central Africa Regional Office) clearly put it, "Mothers-in-law play a key role in infant and child feeding. Mothers-in-law are thought to know better than the [young] mothers how to raise children. They also demand respect, and a good daughter-in-law should follow her advice or else she would be blamed" (2012, 6).

the ways the disease can be transmitted and prevented often do not protect themselves during intercourse (Dolcini, Canin, Gandelman, and Skolnik 2004). It has been pointed out that this "paradox" could be understood by studying the role played by social factors in adopting preventive practices (Gausset 2001). Established social norms about sexuality, gender stereotypes, as well as shared beliefs about causes of illness shape the way people behave in sexual relationships.

All the practices we are trying to improve are steeped in thick webs of beliefs (factual and normative), shared values, customs and norms. How to confirm whether what appears to be a social norm is in fact one is by no means an easy task. Unfortunately, most of the commonly used research surveys do not collect the right information that is needed for the identification of social norms. For example, surveys like the Demographic Health Survey (DHS) only gather data that measure prevalent behaviors within and across communities in a country and across several developing countries. To understand *why* some populations are at risk requires an understanding of the social and cultural factors that support harmful practices. Knowledge, Attitude, and Practice (KAP) surveys often complement DHS data, since they are explicitly designed to uncover these socio-cultural factors that contribute to the target behavioral patterns, be they exclusive breastfeeding, condom use, or otherwise.

KAP surveys measure the knowledge of participants in a domain of interest, their attitudes toward behavior involved in that domain, and their practices with respect to that domain.[2] In the case of exclusive breastfeeding of newborns (the area of interest), knowledge is evaluated by asking participants questions about their factual understanding of breastfeeding, its advantages, drawbacks, et cetera. Yet assessing whether participants'

2. For articles detailing the KAP methodology, as well as discussing its limits, it is instructive to look at the following USAID document—pdf.usaid.

knowledge is consistent with current biomedical knowledge is quite different from learning how the *local knowledge* about breastfeeding is linked to general factual beliefs about milk, water, food, and children's wellbeing (Launiala 2009). It is local knowledge that should be understood and evaluated.

For example, Yoder (1995) demonstrated that local Zairian understandings of the nature, causes, and appropriate treatment of childhood diarrhea differed considerably from the contemporary biomedical approach. What most Westerners would consider a case of diarrhea could be classified as one of six different diseases by residents of Lubumbashi, Zaire, depending on the perceived symptoms of the sufferer. All of the diseases feature frequent stools as one of their central symptoms, but only *Kauhara* (one of the local terms for a type of diarrhea) was functionally equated with what a medical practitioner would diagnose as diarrhea. Other diarrheal classifications, such as *Lukunga*, which featured a "clacking sound"[3] in the mouth as a critical symptom (in addition to frequent stools), was not equated with the typical medical diagnosis. When various organizations tried to inform Zairians about appropriate treatments for diarrhea, many locals likely interpreted the information to be only specific to *Kauhara* (and not other local disease classifications). In line with this assertion, the sampled Zairians in Yoder's (1995) study readily gave the appropriate treatment (e.g., oral rehydration therapy) to their children if they were thought to have *Kahuara* but not if they were thought to have another diarrheal disease. Wrongly assuming that a particular population holds a set of factual beliefs that are consistent with one's own can lead to the design of an ineffective and culturally uninformed intervention, as has been the case in Zaire.

gov/pdf_docs/PNADR956.pdf—as well as to Schopper, Doussantousse, and Orav 1993.

3.  This is a sign of extreme thirst.

From UNICEF participants in our training program I learned that in many parts of Africa milk is classified as "hot" and water "cold," that honored guests are given water, and that children are treated like honored guests. In some communities, children are prevented from eating eggs, as it is believed that a child who eats eggs will become a thief. The colorful stories I heard and Yoder's study on local diagnoses of diarrhea make it clear how important it is to know the local beliefs that often constitute a barrier to change, and how KAP surveys should be enhanced with questions that use ethnographic data (Stycos 1981).

KAP surveys also measure attitudes toward specific behaviors, and assess current practices with questions regarding behavior. Measuring attitudes presents a series of difficulties. First, attitudes are notoriously difficult to define in a precise, operational way, and their correlation with behavior is shaky (Bicchieri and Muldoon 2011). Because of this, I much prefer to measure personal normative beliefs, which have more specific content, and to carefully distinguish between prudential and non-prudential beliefs. One may approve of hand-washing because of its hygienic value (prudential), but also because it is impolite to handshake with dirty hands (non-prudential). Another important consideration in any measurement is that participants may provide survey workers with what they feel is a socially desirable answer, rather than with the answer that reflects their true attitude. This problem is also present when we measure personal normative beliefs.[4] A social desirability bias can also be present when eliciting social expectations. Especially in small and close-knit communities, people may be reluctant to admit that their community is doing something undesirable in the eyes of the surveyor.

Another major problem in assessing social expectations is that reported expectations may not be accurate, in that responders do not have an incentive to seriously guess what others do

4. I have discussed some promising methods to assess personal normative beliefs and obtain truthful answers elsewhere (Bicchieri, Lindemans,

(especially if the behavior is private) and what others approve or disapprove of. In this case, there might be a tendency to project one's own preferences and beliefs. A solution that should be effective in both experimental and field settings is to incentivize the elicitation of empirical and normative expectations. When accurate responses hold the promise of a reward, respondents are motivated to make an accurate guess. Bicchieri, Lindemans, and Jiang (2014) discuss how such incentives for accuracy provide extra motivation even in cases where there is a desire to present one's community in a favorable light.

In my definition of social norms, a key component is the presence of normative expectations. When assessing how much a population approves of a practice, we should not only measure people's personal normative beliefs about the practice, but also their normative expectations about it (asking about how many of their peers approve of it). Though we may have difficulties in incentivizing truthful personal normative beliefs, we can (and do) incentivize accuracy in assessing normative expectations. For example, getting a reward for accuracy encourages serious reflection about what behavior most people in one's community find acceptable or even mandatory. Such methods could be employed to determine if a social norm is in place and how strong it is.

An independent elicitation of social expectations should always accompany observation of behavior. Assessing practices and identifying behavioral patterns is a useful starting point, but much more needs to be done before one can uncover their true nature. Observing actual behavior is obviously important, but it is difficult to infer that a social norm exists from observations alone. First, some social norms are proscriptive: they tell us what not to do. If the norm is effective, the proscribed behavior will

and Jiang 2014), as it is possible to estimate the actual prevalence of personal normative beliefs that, say, support a target practice, without needing to know the true belief state of each individual respondent (Greenberg, Abul-Ela, Simmons, and Horvitz 1969).

not be observed, at least in a setting where the decision makers believe their behavior can be monitored. Second, a stable pattern of behavior may be due to what individuals believe would happen if they deviated from the underlying behavioral rule. Such beliefs are not observable, nor are they inferable from observed actions. We need an assessment of the social norm likely to be in place that is *independent* of the observed behavior.

The theory of norms I introduced in the first chapter can provide guidance in diagnosing with some precision the nature of the behavioral patterns we observe (Figure 2.1). Let us recall the diagnostic diagram:

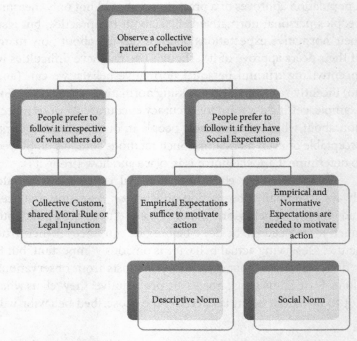

FIGURE 2.1 Diagnostic process of identifying collective behaviors.
Source: C. Bicchieri, *Social Norms, Social Change*. Penn-UNICEF Lecture, July 2012.

The diagram shows that social expectations, or lack thereof, determine whether an observed practice is independent or interdependent and (if so) what sort of interdependence it is. We have seen that customs are held in place because they fulfill some perceived individual need; expectations are not a factor in supporting them. Shared moral or religious codes also affect collective behaviors, but the main reason to follow such codes of conduct is frequently independent of what one observes others doing. Finally, legal injunctions may generate uniform behavior but, again, one has reason to obey the law independently of what others do.

As opposed to independent practices, descriptive and social norms are supported by social expectations, unilateral or multilateral, within a reference network. For a convention like driving on the right side of the road, mutual empirical expectations will suffice to keep us following it. For a social norm of fairness, reciprocal empirical *and* normative expectations are needed for the norm to survive. With a convention such as traffic rules, self-interest depends on *everyone* doing the same thing. Fairness on the other hand may not be in one's immediate self-interest. In anonymous encounters, like many Internet commercial transactions, there is the temptation to cheat (especially if others behave honestly). Normative expectations often keep us honest, either because they involve sanctions or simply because we consider others' expectations of fairness to be legitimate.

Though norm identification may be a daunting task in real-life cases, where we face intricate webs of beliefs, values, and norms, it proves to be a much simpler task in experimental games, where we can present participants with relatively plain, anonymous choices. In a lab experiment, we can easily manipulate the players' environment, elicit the beliefs of participants in various information conditions, and measure the degree to which beliefs affect actual behavior. Norm identification in simple games offers guidance about how to proceed in more complex real-life situations, and helps to uncover the important elements we should pay attention to in order to predict that a norm, if it exists, will in fact be followed. Lest the reader comes to the conclusion that norm identification is all there is to norm measurement, a warning is in order: identifying a norm, and measuring consensus about its relevance in a specific situation, does not guarantee that the norm is followed by all or even most participants. A measure of normative consensus or agreement is different from a measure of compliance, or the conditions under which a norm is likely to be followed. We need both measures to be able to say that a norm exists and is regularly conformed to by members of a relevant reference network. Once we have concluded that a norm exists and that it is the main motivational force driving individuals' behavior, we can feel confident that any interventions aimed at changing the norm will not be in vain.

Before investigating norms and their measurement in a natural setting, that is, "in the wild," let us first look at work that has already been done in a laboratory setting. Here we can back up what we believe to be a true model of social norms with empirical evidence. In the conrolled setting of a laboratory, it is easy to isolate causal variables and perform meaningful manipulations. If there is indeed a norm, then manipulating individuals' expectations (normative or empirical) should change their behavior in predictable ways. Behavioral experiments, with their simplified settings, provide the clarity and guidance of simple but powerful methodological tools.

## NORMS AND GAMES: THE LIMITS OF OBSERVATION

An array of experimental games have been used in research, but only a few are relevant for the investigation of social norms. In many such games, someone can decide how to divide a sum of money between herself and somebody else. In Dictator games, the "dictator" decides such an allocation and that is the end of it. However, in Ultimatum games, the other player gets the opportunity either to accept the proposer's "ultimatum offer" or to reject it, in which case nobody gets anything. Additionally, in Trust games, an "investor" can send money to a "trustee" with whom she is paired, and the trustee can decide whether to reciprocate. In Social Dilemma games, players must decide whether to contribute some money to produce a public good where it is individually rational not to contribute, but everyone is better off if all contribute. Experimental economists typically let their subjects play such games for real money in the controlled environment of the lab.

Social norms are widely invoked to explain data that are difficult if not impossible to explain with alternative theories of behavior. Camerer and Fehr (2002, 92), for example, maintain that deviations from game-theoretic predictions based on self-interest are "naturally interpreted as evidence of social norms." As I mentioned before, merely observing behavior does not justify an inference about the existence of a social norm that would explain that behavior. Additionally, behavioral experiments usually lack a clear, operational definition of what a social norm is, and are thus based on an empty concept from which no sensible prediction can be drawn.

We can interpret experimental evidence of punishment in economic games as evidence that social norms are present, because the violation of a norm typically elicits negative sanctions. We should, however, distinguish second-party from third-party punishment, as they may be differently motivated. Second-party punishment is the costly punishment of one or more players by a player who has a stake in the game. When responders reject low offers in Ultimatum games, these actions can be construed as punishments of unfair proposals.

Second-party punishment may be motivated by anger, resentment, reputation or deterrence effects, moralistic aggression, imagined or real social pressure, or a combination of some of the above. We cannot tell, just by observing punishing behavior, what *motivates* players to punish. To conclude that second-party punishment indicates the presence of social norms is premature.

In third-party punishment, some of the above-mentioned motivations are likely to be absent. Third-party punishment is punishment by an individual who has no monetary interest in the game, and is just an external observer of what other players did. As has been shown experimentally by Fehr and Fischbacher (2004), third-party observers are prepared to punish offenders, but even in this case, we cannot unambiguously state the kind of norm (moral or social) that guides behavior.[5]

Jason Dana and I surveyed 126 undergraduates, asking them to estimate the frequency and judge the fairness or unfairness of a range of possible divisions of $10 in a Dictator game (Bicchieri 2006, 137). A majority (56 percent) thought that keeping all the $10 would be the most common choice and that no offer was unfair, whereas a sizable minority (44 percent) thought that a variety of divisions other than ($10, $0) would be common. When asked whether they would punish offers that they thought unacceptable, very few of those who felt no choice was unfair chose to punish at least one offer, whereas most of the participants who found some offers to be unfair were prepared to punish at least some of them. There was a clear split between those who considered all allocations acceptable and those who instead drew a clear line. Further analysis revealed that responders were more likely to punish an offer that violated what they thought was commonly done than one that offended their sense of fairness. The conclusion we drew is that

5.  Also see Fehr and Gachter (2000).

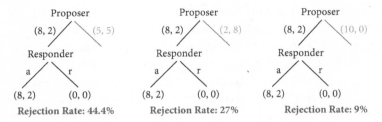

FIGURE 2.2 Three Ultimatum games. Source: Falk et al. 2003.

punishment in Dictator games is not symptomatic of a collectively shared norm of fairness.[6]

As I mentioned earlier, we cannot draw any conclusion about the presence of a social norm or, more generally, about what motivates actors to act as they do, just by observing behavior in a single game. However, by observing behavior in similar games, we may eliminate some hypotheses about players' possible motives. For example, one may test whether players are averse to inequality by presenting players with a series of simple Ultimatum games, where the proposer must choose between two possible alternatives, one of which is constant across games (Falk, Fehr, and Fischbacher 2003). The constant alternative is $8 for the proposer and $2 for the responder, while the second alternative varies by treatment ($5, $5; or $2, $8; or $10, $0). Figure 2.2 is a summary of the rejection rates for each of the three different Ultimatum games in which the proposer offered $2:[7]

When the ($8, $2) offer is compared to the ($5, $5) alternative, the rejection rate is 44.4 percent, much higher than

6. For a discussion of Dictator games and fairness norms, see Guala and Mittone (2010).
7. In the game trees, "a" stands for accept and "r" stands for reject. In each pair of payoffs (in parentheses), the first (left) is the payoff of the proposer and the second (right) is the responder's payoff.

the rejection rates in each of the other treatments. In fact, the rejection rate depends on what the alternative is. The rejection rate decreases to 27 percent if the alternative is ($2, $8), and further decreases to 9 percent if the alternative is ($10, $0). A possible explanation for rejecting an unequal payoff is inequity aversion—a dislike of unequal distributions. Since inequity aversion is usually treated as a stable disposition, responders would be expected to reject an offer of $2 with the same frequency across games. This example, which shows different rejection rates based on the alternatives available to the proposer, suggests that inequity aversion can at best be treated as one among several motivating factors and can be overruled by other considerations.

When explaining behavior in the above series of Ultimatum games, we are tempted to say that the high rejection rate observed when the second alternative is ($5, $5) is due to the fact that responders are being focused on a norm of fairness, whose violation triggers an angry response. This explanation presupposes that presenting responders with a "fair" alternative prompts expectations that are perceived as *legitimate*, or their violation would not provoke a punitive reaction. Rejection follows from violation of what we think are reasonable expectations. This Ultimatum game nicely exemplifies how varying the design of a game can eliminate possible alternative explanations. However, by itself, this experiment does not provide sufficient evidence of norm-driven behavior.

An explanation that relies on norms *presupposes* the existence of social expectations that support the norm, but usually no attempt is made to gauge their existence (if any) and magnitude. Indirectly deriving the norms that might be at work from participants' choices is hopelessly circular: we want to explain behavior by invoking a norm, but we then infer the norm from that very behavior. We must provide independent evidence that a norm exists and is perceived as relevant to the situation by participants. We are faced with a similar circularity when we observe persistent, collective patterns of behavior that we are quick to dub "social norms." Child marriage, female genital cutting, domestic violence, corruption, teenage drinking and risky sexual behavior, to name just a few, are all treated as similar cases of damaging norms, but are they really social norms? The question is not academic: understanding the nature of these practices allows us to design specific, appropriate interventions. Information campaigns may change a custom, but they alone will never change a social norm. Here, too, we need to gather evidence regarding the nature of these practices, and the expectations that support them.

## CONDITIONAL PREFERENCES, SOCIAL EXPECTATIONS

The first step to introduce norms in the explanation of behavior must be a specification of what a norm *is*. There are many definitions in the literature (Bicchieri and Muldoon 2011), but apart from my own, none of them are operational, in the sense of allowing us to identify the conditions under which a norm exists, as well as the conditions under which it is followed. An operational definition is also one that suggests ways to identify norms independently of observed behavior. Let me briefly summarize what I take to be the conditions for a social norm to exist (Bicchieri 2006, 11):

A norm is a behavioral rule that

1. is known to exist and apply to a class of situations,
2. is followed by individuals in a population on condition that

a. it is believed that sufficiently many others follow it (empirical expectations), and

b. it is believed that sufficiently many others believe the rule should be followed, and/or may be willing to sanction deviations from it (normative expectations).

This definition entails that compliance with a norm is *conditional* on having the right kind of expectations. It follows that a norm may exist and not be followed at a given time if empirical and/or normative expectations are not present. A typical case of failure of empirical expectations would look like this: you come to realize that many of your neighbors, who you believed consistently paid their dues for the common garden, have discontinued payments. You then conclude it is time to stop your payments for the time being, even if your conviction that everyone *should* contribute (your personal normative belief) is unabated. Your empirical expectations have changed, leading to a change in behavior. It may also happen that normative expectations will not likely lead to any negative sanctions: You are a proposer in a typical Ultimatum game and are told that responders believe that a random device will determine their offer. Now you are pretty sure that your responder will not expect an equal outcome, since he believes chance determines what he gets. For the same reason, you expect the responder will probably accept any offer. The responder does not have an expectation about what he *should* be offered, since he thinks there is no good or bad intention behind what he gets. Even if you are normally bent on choosing a fair division (in part to avoid the risk of punishment), you may be tempted to keep all the money, since the risk of punishment is absent (Bicchieri and Chavez 2013). It might also be argued that this is a case where the normative expectation has changed. The proposer may believe that the responder, convinced that the outcome is the result of a random device, believes that any outcome that results from a fair process is fair.

The conditional aspect of following a norm differentiates a norm-based explanation from those that employ the concept of social or moral preference. Conforming to a social norm of fairness is different from endorsing fairness: I may conform to a fairness rule if I have beliefs about what others who are relevant to me do and approve of, but I may care little about fairness per se. I conditionally prefer to be fair, but I may not have an unconditional preference for fairness. In social preference models, the disposition to be fair is assumed to be a stable disposition, and variations in behavior are difficult to explain within that framework.[8] A conditional preference account instead offers the possibility of empirically testing if a change in expectations induces predictable changes in behavior. Were the expectations that support a norm to be different, we would predict behavior to change in specific directions. As we shall see, this consideration is crucial in guiding field measurements, where we want to assess whether a practice is a social norm and, if so, which expectations matter to its survival.

## NORM IDENTIFICATION: ELICITING EXPECTATIONS

Having defined what a norm is (a behavioral rule supported by mutual empirical and normative expectations and conditional preferences), we must show that in fact a norm *exists* for the individuals in a specific situation. After all, in order

8. For a discussion of different types of social preferences, and how conditional preferences differ from them, see Bicchieri and Zhang (2012).

to comply with a norm, one must be aware of it and believe that this particular situation is one to which a norm applies. *We*, the researcher or intervention designer, may think that a norm of fairness is elicited in an Ultimatum game, but this may not be the case. We should not *presuppose* that behavior is norm-guided, even when we have a strong sense that it might be. We must prove that indeed participants have the appropriate normative expectations, and that those expectations are mutually consistent. This does not guarantee that a norm, if it exists, will always be followed; it will just tell us that players know it exists and applies to their situation. Armed with this knowledge, we can then test when expectations influence behavior and when they do not, and check under which information conditions a norm will be followed.

The first and most important step in norm identification is thus an *independent assessment* of individual expectations. Using questionnaires allows us to measure personal normative beliefs and empirical and normative expectations, as well as to check for their internal consistency. Questionnaires are also the tool of choice to find out whether participants in experiments are aware that a specific norm applies to their situation, as well as to measure consensus about the salience of the norm in that situation. A problem with questionnaires is that responders do not have a particular incentive to be sincere, accurate, or think seriously about the question. This is why experimental economists prefer to observe people's behavior in games for real money. Since we cannot observe beliefs, we must rely on incentivized behavior. Yet we have seen that the same behavior can stem from many different beliefs, and we have no way to tell beliefs apart unless we ask. There seems to be a dilemma: either properly incentivize behavior or be content with unreliable cognitive information.

Another related problem has to do with "experimenter demand effects" (Rosenthal 1976; Zizzo 2010): responders may want to say things that they believe will please the experimenter. While anonymizing answers (removing information that identifies the responder) should solve this problem, full anonymity, especially informing and convincing subjects of it, is difficult to achieve in practice. Some degree of experimenter demand effect might be inevitable after all. Moreover, according to self-image maintenance theory, even in fully anonymous situations, subjects might still answer in a biased way to maintain a good self-image, which remains a validity problem for un-incentivized questionnaires. Thus, it is all the more important to pay or remunerate subjects in other ways for their accurate answers to alleviate the problem when eliciting their social expectations. Cognitive information can and should be incentivized.

What sort of questions should be asked? Depending on the context, we may want to gauge all or a combination of the following:[9]

1. *Personal normative beliefs*: Do you believe $x$ is fair, appropriate, . . .? Should $x$ be chosen?
2. *Empirical expectations* (incentivized): How many participants do you think choose $x$? What do you think most participants will/did choose? What do you think the majority of participants will/did choose? If your guess is correct, you earn a $y$\$ bonus.
3. *Normative expectations*[10] (incentivized): Guess how many (most, a majority of, . . . .) other participants believe $x$ is fair, appropriate, should be chosen, etc. If your guess is correct, you earn a $y$\$ bonus.

---

9. Each question can be repeated for each option available to the participants.
10. Note that normative expectations are second-order normative beliefs (i.e., I believe that others believe that one should/should not . . . ).

The following Table 2.1 summarizes the kind of beliefs we may want to assess.[11]

Table 2.1

**A SUMMARY OF PERSONAL AND SOCIAL BELIEFS**

| *What one believes about* | *Self* | *Others* | *Others 2nd order* |
|---|---|---|---|
| EMPIRICAL | What I am going to do | What others do (empirical expectation) | What others believe I/others do |
| NORMATIVE | What I should do (personal normative belief) | What others should do (personal normative belief) | What others believe I/others should do (normative expectation) |

When a social norm exists and applies to a specific situation, the normative expectations of participants will be mutually consistent. This means that most participants believe that most other participants think that a specific rule of behavior should be followed in that situation. Note that to identify a norm it is not necessary to question the participants in an experimental game. We may also ask third parties to observe the results of one or more games, and elicit both their personal beliefs about appropriate behavior, as well as their second-order beliefs about what most other third

11.  To identify social norms, we usually only need to gauge personal normative beliefs and empirical/normative expectations, but on occasion we may also want to evaluate second-order empirical expectations, as when we ask people not just what they or others would do, but also what they think others believe people in their situation would (as opposed to should) do.

parties think is appropriate behavior (normative expectations). In this case, too, mutual consistency of normative expectations tells us there is probably a norm, and is relevant to that setting.

Mutual consistency of normative expectations is only a necessary condition for identifying a social norm, not a sufficient one. People share prudential, moral, and religious norms that are only *social* in a weak sense, since believing that the behavior is commonly adopted and that people approve of it does not constitute a reason for following it. Let me give some examples of shared prudential and moral norms:

1. Personal normative belief: I think one should not smoke.
2. Normative expectation: I believe the majority of people in my reference network think one should not smoke.
3. Empirical expectation: Most people in my reference network do not smoke.

Here we may face a shared norm, but is it a social norm? Individuals who hold these beliefs may think that smoking is a bad habit that should be avoided and share this conviction, but are only motivated to avoid smoking by a prudential reason: it is bad for one's health. The fact that they share a prudential belief does not imply that their choice is influenced by their social expectations. Their preferences are not socially conditional: they would prefer not to smoke no matter what.

Let us now consider a shared moral norm:

1. Personal normative belief: I think one should not harm innocent people.
2. Normative expectation: I believe most people in my reference network believe that one should not harm innocent people.
3. Empirical expectation: Most people in my reference network do not harm innocent people.

Again, we may face a shared norm, but are people motivated to avoid harming innocents because they believe this is an uncommon behavior, and moreover a behavior that is condemned by most? The fact that they share a moral belief does not imply that their choice is influenced by their social expectations. Their preferences are not socially conditional: they would prefer not to harm innocents no matter what.

A social norm is different from a shared prudential or moral norm because it involves (socially) conditional preferences. Eliciting social expectations and finding there is a consensus on "what should be done" does not make a shared norm a *social* one. There are, however, ways to disentangle the prudential from the moral or social. Since norm transgression usually triggers some form of negative sanction, a further way to check for the presence of shared moral or social norms is to ask whether a specific behavior elicits condemnation or punishment. Ignoring prudential norms does not trigger punishment: we may think that drinking and eating to excess, smoking, and being a couch potato are damaging behaviors and try to convince our family and friends to change their ways, but there is no condemnation or punishment. They are just harming themselves and we may feel sorry for them.

It is also important to realize that we cannot establish that there is a shared norm only by asking people whether *they* would punish deviant behavior. Depending upon their personal values, some would punish no matter what, and others would not. Some may feel a deep personal allegiance to a norm, whereas others may just abide by it in the right circumstances, but evade it whenever possible, and thus look upon transgressors with indulgence. If we instead ask participants what they expect *others* to do (e.g., will most people punish?), then we have a better idea of what sort of behavior is socially or morally required, provided individuals' expectations are in agreement (Bicchieri, Xiao, and Muldoon 2011). Only when there is such a consensus are we justified in claiming that a norm exists, and that people are aware of it.

Once more, the shared norm may not be a social one: We may be willing to punish those who harm the innocent, but refrain from harming because we morally condemn those acts, not because we might face punishment and condemnation. These may not be conditional preferences, just shared unconditional ones. The relevance of this consideration is not merely academic. There are cultures in which codes of honor and purity are widely shared, and govern behaviors that we may find unacceptable, like female genital cutting or honor killing. If we want to promote change, it is important to understand whether individuals conform to the code *because* of their social expectations, or simply because they all happen to embrace similar ideals of honor and purity.

Asking participants whether others would punish deviant behavior is a step forward in disentangling the prudential from the moral or social, but we need more than that to uncover social norms. Nevertheless, it is still interesting to ask participants whether *they* would punish the transgression. The comparison between the subjects' own personal opinions about the gravity of transgressing and their beliefs about others' opinions will capture the distance between perceived and objective consensus. Pluralistic ignorance, a belief trap examined in chapter 1, is an example of such a divergence: we may think we are the sole "deviants" when in fact most people think like us, but we have no way to communicate our real opinions. With no transparent communication, a norm that is only weakly supported, if at all, will endure unchallenged. Fortunately, the bigger the difference between objective and perceived consensus, the easier it might be to change a harmful or inefficient social norm. I say "social," and not moral or religious norm, because pluralistic ignorance only matters for social norms. With a moral norm, I may be wrongly convinced that most people embrace it, but were their true beliefs revealed, I would not budge in my conviction about what is the moral thing to do.

To summarize: to identify a norm we need to establish that there is consensus about what actions are appropriate/inappropriate in what situations. This can be done in a variety of ways. We may ask what actions people tend to punish and check for mutual consistency of *empirical* expectations. We may also directly elicit personal normative beliefs about specific actions, measure second-order beliefs about what *others* believe is appropriate/inappropriate, and check for mutual consistency of *normative* expectations. The latter is the method of choice to detect pluralistic ignorance. After collecting personal normative beliefs, we can easily measure whether participants' second-order beliefs are correct. Perceived consensus and objective consensus may differ, and when second-order beliefs are mutually consistent but systematically inaccurate, we know that people uphold a norm they dislike. If their doubts are not shared, the norm will persist.

Yet we are still far from able to claim that the shared norm is a social one. The next step is to check whether preferences are conditional on social expectations. In other words, are individuals motivated to act by what others (that are relevant to them) do and believe should be done? Is there a causal link between expectations and behavior?

## IS THIS A SOCIAL NORM? THE ROLE OF CONDITIONAL PREFERENCES

As I mentioned at the outset, a social norm is characterized by social expectations and conditional preferences. The presence of social expectations is not sufficient to conclude there is a social norm. These expectations must also motivate individuals to follow the norm. In other words, we must have a conditional preference for conforming to the norm, given those social expectations. This is what makes social norms different from shared moral, religious, or prudential norms. This is also what makes social and descriptive norms similar: the only difference is that normative expectations play a causal role in social norms, but not in descriptive norms.

How can we be sure that preferences are in fact conditional? In other words, how do we know that social expectations, even if present, matter to choice? The only way to know is to *manipulate* social expectations, and check if behavior changes in predictable ways. Again, experimental games are a useful starting point, since they let us manipulate players' expectations in a controlled way to assess (a) whether we face a real social norm, and (b) under which conditions the norm will be obeyed or evaded (such as by varying the information we give to the players). At least for the population under study, systematic deviations from a norm we have identified measure how much individuals care about what the norm stands for, or their sensitivity to it. Sensitivity to a norm is inversely related to the relative influence of one's social expectations in motivating compliance. The greater the proportion of a reference network that one expects to have personal normative beliefs endorsing a behavior, and the stronger one expects such beliefs to be, the more weight one will assign to those beliefs when making a decision. Even if we do not care much about a norm, strong normative expectations (and the accompanying threat of sanctions) will induce us to comply. Conversely, the more we value a norm, the less we worry about how many people follow it or how keenly they monitor our actions. Nevertheless, even if we care about a social norm, we still take into account others' behaviors and beliefs when making decisions, though to a lesser degree. In both cases, preferences are conditional, since social expectations are necessary to induce conforming behavior, but the motivational power of expectations will vary.

There are circumstances in which individuals may be tempted to skirt a norm they know applies to the situation. I am not talking about those who would regularly evade existing norms. Such people exist, but they are a minority. I am interested in those who would obey a norm under the right conditions, but otherwise flout it. A common example is the presence of ambiguities that can be exploited to one's advantage. When facing several possible norms, or alternative interpretations of the same norm, self-serving norm manipulation frequently occurs. In other cases, we may face divergent expectations, or even realize that some expectations are just not there. In these cases, norm evasion becomes frequent. Let us look at both phenomena more closely, keeping in mind that in all these cases we will need some independent measure of empirical and normative expectations.

## WHAT TO DO WITH NORMS: MANIPULATION

### (a) Multiple Norms

We often face situations where more than one norm applies. People who abide by honor norms also hold norms of protective parenting. In the 1960s, Sicily was a place where honor norms held strong. For example, a girl who was raped was expected to marry her rapist to preserve her family's honor. In the well-known case of Franca Viola, this expectation was completely reframed. She was raped but refused to marry her rapist, and her unusual decision was supported by her father, who put caring for and protecting his child above the powerful norm of honor. By appealing to this other norm, he was able to justifiably defy honor norms.

The conflict between different norms is something we experience frequently. We may want to cooperate with strangers, but also feel loyalty to our own group. We may want to reciprocate a gift, but what if the act of "giving back" creates an inequality that favors the other party? Erte Xiao and I (2010) devised an experiment to check if indeed—when we pit equality against reciprocity—self-serving norm manipulation occurs. We designed two Trust games: in one the players started with equal endowments, and in the other, the investor had double the endowment of the trustee. In both cases, the investor could choose to transfer a fixed amount of money to the trustee or keep it all. The trustee who received the money could keep it all or transfer back any amount to the investor. In the equal endowment condition, the modal behavior was to return half of what was received. Reciprocity was the main consideration. In the second condition, where players started out with unequal amounts, if the investor transferred the fixed amount, she achieved equality, with each player ending up with the same amount. If the trustee sent nothing back, equality was preserved. If she transferred anything, she reciprocated but created an inequality. The initially unequal condition is one we commonly encounter in the workplace and when exchanging favors and gifts, where reciprocity may be impaired by an inequality of initial endowments. We observed that in this condition a majority of trustees kept all the money. Self-interest and equality bonded in crowding out reciprocity. As the interests of investors and trustees were not fully aligned, it is not surprising that trustees supported equality when it was in their interest to demand equality, and otherwise backed reciprocity. A simple conclusion is that individuals display a selfish, self-serving bias, favoring the rule that best serves their interests. Yet the literature on motivated reasoning[12] suggests a more complex reading of this behavior (Kunda 1990; Mercier and Sperber 2011). Self-serving biases often occur when

12. Motivated reasoning is a cognitive bias that drives individuals to seek out evidence that supports conclusions that they find agreeable,

a choice can be *publicly justified* as reasonable, if not optimal for all of the parties.[13] We rationalize our behaviors, but the reasons must pass muster with the relevant audience.

To test our hypothesis, we looked to uninvolved third parties, asking them to judge the trustee's behavior in both conditions. Results (Bicchieri and Mercier 2013) showed that third parties sided with the trustees in agreeing that it was more important to restore equality than to reciprocate (at least when inequality is not strongly justified). In other words, the trustees' behavior was justified by third parties. Despite the fact that the trustees were selective in their norm adherence in a selfish way, they were ultimately choosing a norm that was publically justifiable.

The case of Franca Viola, who was supported by her family in refusing to engage in *matrimonio riparatore* (a "rehabilitating marriage"), is a real-life example of norm manipulation. Her family's actions could be publically justifiable by stressing the importance of caring for and protecting one's child. Few people could object to that.

Life is rife with situations in which different, sometimes incompatible norms may apply. Think of a family who endorses strong norms of purity that result in practices such as female genital cutting. The same family may hold strong norms that dictate protection of one's child, especially avoiding harming that child. Both norms are prima facie publically justifiable. As I discuss in chapters 3 and 4, an important tool of norm change is collective discussion about the norms we uphold and how they fit with other norms and values that we hold dear. As in the case of equality and reciprocity,

---

typically those that are aligned with their preexisting beliefs and preferences.

13. See Valdesolo and DeSteno (2008) for a discussion of rationalizing behaviors.

purity and the avoidance of bodily harm may initially hold the same weight, but through the process of discussion, people may come to realize that they may be incompatible, and that protection of one's child (in the sense of avoiding harming him or her) carries more weight than the need for purity, as attained through female genital cutting. The same norm manipulation that people do on their own can be elicited through other means, such as collective discussions about norms, values, and beliefs. Once it is accepted that certain norms of purity are not compatible with the goal of not inflicting harm, it becomes much more difficult to publically justify them.

## (b) Multiple Interpretations

Often we do not face different norms, but just different interpretations of the same norm. Many pro-social norms, such as fairness, reciprocity, and cooperation, are subject to multiple interpretations. Think of fairness: we can divide according to need, merit, or just implement an equal division. It comes as no surprise that people try to steer a division in their favor if they have a good argument to support their greater share. Sometimes the *object* to be divided is the bone of contention. Think of climate negotiations. China and other emerging nations want an equity principle that relies on historical carbon output (a carbon stock story). The United States and Western Europe want an equity principle that relies on current per capita output (a carbon flows approach). These are both self-serving—China wants the stocks account to mitigate against the fact that it is currently the biggest polluter. The West wants the flows account because most of the stock is from the West. There is a good moral gloss on each thought, and there is an ambiguity about what fairness should mean here. In domestic politics, we see political speakers try to use their favored interpretation to gain support for their policies. Fairness is used both to argue for spending more on social security and to disband it. Between the Tea Party and the Occupy movement, there are plenty of attempts to appropriate fairness norms for personal political ends. People may choose to believe that what they prefer is publically justifiable and acceptable, or they may just choose the option that they personally favor. Being able to assess both personal normative beliefs and normative expectations should allow us to disentangle these two kinds of self-serving choices.

As far as I can tell, the only experiments aimed at checking the nature of norm manipulation were those I did with Alex Chavez at Penn in 2009 (Bicchieri and Chavez 2010). We measured the existence and pertinence of social norms through incentivized questionnaires, so there could be no doubt that participants knew what norm(s) applied to their situation, and were reasonably sure that other participants, by and large, saw the situation as they did. We also manipulated information in order to change players' expectations, to check whether behavior would change, too.

In our variant of the Ultimatum game, the proposer chose from one of the three following options: ($5, $5), ($8, $2), or Coin (in which case one of the other two allocations was randomly selected). In this case, we presented two ways to conceive of fairness: as an equal outcome ($5, $5) or as a fair procedure (Coin). We surveyed all players' normative expectations about those offers that they believed were considered fair by most responders. If their estimation was accurate, players were awarded a monetary prize. We discovered that normative expectations were mutually consistent. Most participants believed that a majority of responders deemed ($5, $5) and Coin (in a smaller, but still quite high, percentage) to be fair and acceptable.

We also created informational asymmetries between proposers and responders. Participants played three Ultimatum games under different information conditions in a within-subjects design. In the *public information condition*, all participants understood that the Coin option was available and that responders would know if the proposer with whom they were paired chose Coin. In the *private information condition*, responders did not know that Coin was available to proposers, and proposers were aware of this fact. In the *limited information condition*, participants knew that the Coin option was available, but that the responder would not be able to distinguish whether the proposer chose ($5, $5) or ($8, $2) directly, or chose Coin whose outcome was ($5, $5) or ($8, $2).

The frequency of Coin selection was highest in the public information condition, when the Coin option was common knowledge, and its result transparent. Here proposers could not ignore normative expectations to make a fair offer, but Coin gave them an advantage over ($5, $5).[14] In subsequent experiments, Alex and I elicited proposers' beliefs to check if proposers were driven by a self-serving bias (Bicchieri and Chavez 2013). The bias did drive beliefs, and we concluded that what appears to be a self-serving bias is rooted in the participants' desire to convince themselves that what benefits them is also fair, and acceptable to those who will bear the consequences of their actions.

Self-serving biases also appear in many unexpected environments. Think of child marriage that is often supported by strong social norms of purity, protection, and gender. In a situation where a monetary incentive has been introduced to keep girls in school until an older age, a family may face a conflict between the desire for the economic incentive or adherence to the traditional practice of child marriage. The availability of monetary incentives may push the father to reinterpret what

14. In our experiment, Coin's expected utility is $3.50 for responders, which is less than the $5 they would get from an equal share.

it means to take care of his daughter. Providing alternatives that are framed in desirable lights is a good tactic for changing behavior.

We may conclude that selective norm adherence is a genuine phenomenon, that ambiguity about which among several norms apply may diminish norm compliance (as I described in the earlier example of eliminating female genital cutting), and that behavior may change when a norm is susceptible to several interpretations (as I described in the earlier example of ending child marriage).[15]

## WHAT TO DO WITH NORMS: VIOLATION AND TRANSGRESSION

Norms can be openly defied, as when someone declines to help in situations in which help is needed or refuses to return a favor that he himself requested. Such people do not care about the harm they cause, or think they can "get away with it" at no cost. Institutions, too, may overtly transgress. Safety regulations are breached by companies that hope their infractions will go undetected, as when chemical waste is dumped into a river, dangerous gases are released into the air, or consumer products are tainted to cut costs. These types of transgression usually occur when sanctions are mild or absent, as the agents in question find it convenient to impose costs on others with little concern for the consequences. Another, very different type of transgression happens when breaching a norm signals one's rejection of what the norm stands for, as the novels of De Sade, Dostoyevsky, or Burgess illustrate. Rebellion involves a breach of social

---

15. Experimental evidence shows that school-age children are also fully capable of manipulating norms, even if they are much less "Machiavellian" than adults. See Castelli et al. 2014.

taboos, be they sex, drugs, or murder, but the villain is proud of his feat, or at least is not burdened by futile scruples, since he despises the norms of the society in which he lives. A different, more benign case of norm transgression is one in which the norm is harmful or maladaptive, but only a small minority of people (i.e., the trendsetters) have the conviction to openly and proudly defy the norm. I will discuss the role of trendsetters in norm change in chapter 5.

Norm evasion is different from transgression, and more interesting, since it involves the deliberate but *hidden* violation of a social norm. Since norm compliance is the result of preferences that are conditional on expectations, evasion occurs when some expectations are absent or plainly inconsistent.[16] In one case, the evader is comforted by the fact that his victim does not know she has been wronged. In the other, there is safety in numbers, as when we realize that bad behavior is quite common and we can hide behind what is commonly done. Let us consider these two cases in turn.

## (a)  Asymmetric Information

We often know more than the party with whom we are interacting. This is common in principal-agent exchanges, in all sorts of markets, and in all personal relations (insofar as we know more about ourselves than our partners or friends). As it happens, we may profit from this asymmetry in that we can cheat without the other party realizing it. An egregious example is found in an experiment by Kagel, Kim, and Moser (1996). In their Ultimatum game, when only proposers knew that the

---

16.  Evasion happens also when we avoid situations where a norm would apply, like crossing the street at the sight of a beggar waiting on our side of the road. If we do not pass by the beggar, we are not compelled to be charitable.

chips to be shared were worth three times as much for them than for the responder, they offered, on average, only half of the chips. In this case, rejections were low (and likely expected to be low). Had the proposers distributed profits equally, they should have offered ¾ of the chips to responders.

Asymmetric information lets proposers evade a norm with impunity. This is exemplified in the previously mentioned Ultimatum game (Bicchieri and Chavez 2010), where proposers could choose between ($5, $5), ($8, $2), or a coin flip that gave an equal chance of getting ($5, $5) or ($8, $2). Proposers believed that a large majority of responders found Coin to be fair, so in a condition when responders only received information about their payoff and could not tell whether the offer was intentional or random, a majority of proposers chose to give only $2. Most responders accepted the offer, probably thinking it was indeed a random outcome. It is clear that normative expectations exist, in that responders are expected to believe that they should be treated fairly, but they can be violated with impunity.[17] The proposer might have had the following train of thought: *I believe the responder thinks that tossing a coin is fair; hence, she expects an outcome determined by chance, not an equal one. If she receives $2, she will not be upset.* Here someone who is normally bent on choosing an equal division may be tempted to keep a larger share, since she is not openly defying the other party's normative expectation.

When a norm is secretly breached, should we conclude that the transgressor's sensitivity to the norm is low? The answer is positive with open transgressions. For someone with low sensitivity, only sanctions will induce compliance. Hidden violations are interesting because they show us that we cannot

---

17. As I mentioned before, it might also be argued that normative expectations have changed, in that responders are believed to think that the outcome of a random process is fair.

exclude that someone, though normally sensitive to fairness, would be unfair if normative expectations were thought to be absent or transgressions were undetectable. In chapter 3, I will discuss how norms may emerge but, to survive, need monitoring and sanctioning. The case of open defecation is a key example; once a village has decided to invest in building and using latrines, individuals may still have the temptation to avoid their use because it is more beneficial (in terms of convenience) for them to do so. Awareness of this temptation leads villagers to monitor and sanction misbehavior in order to discourage transgressions. Without monitoring, the new norm of latrine use could be secretly breached, even if the transgressor is convinced that latrines are a good idea. Remember: we are not talking of unconditional norms that we follow no matter what. Social norms are more complex in that we *conditionally* prefer to follow them. If someone does not know what we are doing, and thus will not feel saddened or angered by what he cannot see, why not cheat a little?

Let us now turn to situations where, even if sensitivity to a norm could have originally been high, receiving conflicting empirical information may lower normative expectations to a point where they carry no weight. As in the case of contributing to the maintenance of a common garden, the hold of a norm that requires sharing the burden may considerably weaken when one realizes that many of those who should pay their dues skirt their duty.

## (b) Conflicting Information

Suppose we let college students know that heavy drinking and date rape are extremely frequent on campus. What are the students hearing? Receiving the message about frequent behavior is likely to indicate that there is some semblance of acceptance of such behavior, at least by the parties who transgress. The updated empirical expectations easily bleed into the normative realm. Disclosing information about how common some "bad" behaviors are is counterproductive. Think of illegally downloading music or television shows. It is rampant, and people vaguely have the feeling that it is wrong, but at the same time, everyone does it. The same goes for bribing or violent behaviors when they are pervasive. We know these behaviors are condemned, but when empirical and normative expectations diverge, people are tempted to follow the crowd, because the normative message loses power, and probably also appeal.

Erte Xiao and I were curious about what happens when people are given conflicting information about what other people in their situation do as opposed to what should be done (Bicchieri and Xiao 2009). Typically, social norms combine descriptive and normative elements: We know what we should do, and we observe people doing the right thing. But what if the messages are inconsistent? Will people change their expectations about what is done in those situations? Will they come to discount the norm? To answer these questions, Erte and I exposed different dictator groups to alternative social histories of beliefs and behaviors. At first, we gave simple and consistent messages. Some told the players what other players did in an identical game (either they made a generous offer or a selfish one). Others told the players what other players said ought to be done in an identical game (either one should make a generous offer or a selfish one). We then measured our dictators' expectations about what other dictators in the *present* experiment would do. It turns out that their expectations were directly influenced by the message they received, regardless of the nature of the message. Those who received the selfish message expected greater selfishness, and those who received the generous message expected greater generosity. Both descriptive messages (what others did) and normative messages (what others said one should do) had a major influence on expectations and subsequent choices *when they were the only message received.*

What happens when the descriptive and the normative diverge? We explored this possibility by subsequently giving our players contradictory messages. For example, we would tell them that a majority of dictators in a previous experiment behaved selfishly, but also that a majority of dictators in a different earlier experiment said that one should make a generous offer. We then checked players' expectations about other players in the present game. We found out that what others did overshadowed normative messages (what others said one should do) in forming individuals' expectations and directing their choices. Examples of bad behavior made positive normative messages worthless. This is a discouraging realization if we hope to change behavior by disseminating normative messages. It is well known that moralizing campaigns have little effect (Mendelsohn 1973). Our experiment tells quite clearly that this lack of influence is due to a divergent and inconsistent observation: most people behave badly. Yet, we have acquired an important piece of information for norm change. Change will result from a change in empirical expectations, since when we realize that most people behave differently the threat of sanctions will disappear. If we recognize that a significant number of people in our reference network are breaching the norm, we will no longer fear punishment for disobeying a norm that may have already been abandoned. I will discuss the importance of changing empirical expectations when abandoning a norm in greater detail in chapter 3.

To summarize: to check whether a social norm exists for the individuals who display a regular, collective pattern of behavior, we have to measure their normative expectations. If these expectations are mutually consistent, in that people collectively agree the behavior is appropriate and expected, then we can say (as a first approximation) that there is a social norm.[18] The final test, however, is one that checks whether preferences are conditional on social expectations. We have to check whether the choice to engage in appropriate behavior is sensitive to expectations and, if such expectations were to change, behavior would change in a predictable direction. We therefore need to measure expectations, "manipulate" them in a controlled way, and check if behavior is sensitive to such manipulation. We have explored how expectations can be measured and how inducing or changing them can subsequently change behavior in a controlled setting. I shall explore in the next section how these methods can be fruitfully applied to more complex, real circumstances outside the laboratory.

## THROUGH THE EYES OF OTHERS

Applying the lessons learned from theoretical and experimental work on social norms to the field is no easy task. The number of factors one has to deal with explodes when leaving the laboratory. There are considerations such as sampling techniques, and survey and vignette design (if one were to employ vignettes) that are critical for implementing an effective behavioral intervention. Here, I want to concentrate on the general lessons that we have learned from our experimental work on social norms and other collective behaviors, and how they can be applied to a field setting. This includes the sorts of questions we need to ask and the main theoretical factors we should keep in mind (e.g., factual beliefs, empirical and normative expectations, proper incentivization,

18. Note that it could also be a religious or moral injunction, but in that case social expectations would not play a causal role.

and the conditionality of preferences) when measuring collective behaviors in the field.

Many of the laboratory experiments I described have proven to be useful tools to test my theory of norms. Through incentivized questionnaires about normative expectations, I have assessed whether a norm exists for the parties involved. These questionnaires measure *perceived consensus*, or the degree of mutual consistency in the participants' normative expectations. Mutual consistency, if present, tells us that there is a consensus regarding what behavior is acceptable in a particular situation. Additionally, I have focused on assessing conditional preferences (and their strength) through inducing or changing social expectations. Even if a norm is present, we should not overestimate the intensity of allegiance to the approved behavior. The existence of conditional preferences tells us that, were expectations to change, behavior would change and norm-compliance may significantly weaken. The techniques for changing or creating expectations that I described are useful ways to measure deviations from the shared norm and to highlight the conditions under which a deviation is likely to occur.

How can we apply what we have learned about identifying and measuring norms in the lab to real-life cases? The general process by which one can identify the nature of a collective behavior does not change from the lab to the field, and gauging the conditions under which a norm will be followed is of no lesser consequence because we are now dealing with untidy realities. Measuring the degree of consensus on the appropriateness of specific behaviors, checking whether social expectations play a causal role in directing choices, and identifying under which conditions people conform to some behaviors remain central to understanding why certain patterns of behavior persist.

In my work with UNICEF, the collective behaviors of interest included common practices such as child marriage, female genital cutting, limited breastfeeding, and open defecation.

These practices produce physical harm and/or long-term socioeconomic damage to their targets. Some of these cases are driven by social norms, others are customs, and yet others seem to be purely descriptive norms, where normative content is absent. Encouraging effective change requires understanding the motives that drive actions, as well as how the actors themselves view their practices. We can still use incentivized surveys to identify shared norms, be they prudential, social, or moral, but we cannot as easily check for conditional preferences using experimental methods similar to the ones I described earlier. In real-life scenarios, we are not dealing with relatively simple pro-social norms, such as fairness or reciprocity, that can still be measured through behavioral experiments in small societies, such as those reported by Henrich and colleagues (2005).[19] When the norm might be "obey your mother-in-law" or "marry off your daughter at a young age," how would we conduct a behavioral experiment? How could we succeed in manipulating information (and expectations) in an environment in which people know very well what others in their reference network do (and will presumably continue to do) and have no good reason to change their beliefs? In this case, we need to use other strategies to test the causal influence of social expectations, though what we learned in the lab remains a good guide about how to proceed.

Since we cannot directly manipulate expectations, as we do in the lab, we have to present people with *hypothetical scenarios* to elicit the normative principles they share, as well as check for the existence of conditional preferences and the respective roles that empirical and normative expectations play

19. Henrich and colleagues (2005) travelled to a diverse set of hunter-gatherer societies around the globe and administered several of the most common economic games to the populace. Their study is one of the few to test these behavioral experiments in small-scale societies.

in decision-making. In a lab experiment, we can change the information conditions, or use social history to induce or change expectations. In the "wild" we could instead ask hypothetical questions, such as "If you learned that . . . what would you do?" Note that hypothetical questions may be difficult to answer, as they require the capability to answer "what if" questions and also imagine scenarios that may seem prima facie impossible. They require the ability to assume as true claims that may conflict with what is accepted as true, and lack of such ability may lead someone to deny that the suggested scenario is possible. It may be easier to answer hypothetical questions about the future (*what if . . . were to do x?*) than counterfactual questions about the past (*what if . . . had not done x?*), or questions about fantasy characters rather than family and friends. We would therefore have to judge whether the individuals interviewed are able to entertain hypothetical or counterfactual scenarios and predict their own and others' behavior in these scenarios. We should be aware that social desirability biases could be at work here since there would be an incentive to answer such questions in a way that is deemed desirable by the researcher or that puts one's group in a favorable light, and therefore we should employ the same incentivizing techniques described earlier in the chapter.

Hypothetical and counterfactual questions are especially important to establish whether respondents have conditional preferences. In laboratory experiments, we alter expectations via messages, social history, or allowing communication before playing the game, and check whether behavior is affected. These experimental manipulations can be approximated in a field setting by asking actors if they would change their usual, socially acceptable behavior if enough of their relevant peers did so, if they were to receive different advice from a trusted source, or if people in their reference network thought they ought to do things differently. As I mentioned earlier, hypothetical and counterfactual questions are not easy to answer directly, and answers are subject to social desirability biases. Because of these problems, I shall discuss the importance of using vignettes later on.

In sum, moving from the lab to the field does not change the importance of measuring consensus, conditional preferences, and compliance, but it significantly changes the tools we use to carry out such measures. As we shall see, surveys and vignettes are the tools of choice. We should either ask questions about both real and hypothetical situations or present individuals with scenarios they have to interpret and evaluate. Surveys, as we shall see, may have other, unintended benefits. When we evaluate collective practices, we want to know the *motives* that drive people to engage in them. As I mentioned in the first chapter, such motives are complex, as they encompass factual and personal normative beliefs, as well as social beliefs, such as empirical and normative expectations. Eliciting such motives is a useful exercise not only for the researcher, but also for the person being questioned: people often have motives that they do not realize they are acting on, so this exercise may make them conscious of why they act as they do. Someone may also behave in a specific way because he does not conceive of alternatives. Families may cut their daughters or marry them off early, because "this is the way we do things here, this is the tradition," and no alternative behavior may be available or imagined. Asking hypothetical questions may make people aware of possible alternatives, a first step toward change. Furthermore, empirical and normative expectations may not be differentiated in people's minds, but they may become more clearly separated by answering questions about them. Note that eliciting factual and personal normative beliefs, empirical expectations, and normative expectations does not require the use of hypothetical scenarios. Hypotheticals and counterfactuals included in surveys or vignettes are only needed to check for the presence of conditional preferences and the conditions under which such preferences would change.

## Factual Beliefs

Any practice we engage in is accompanied by factual beliefs about it. People who practice open defecation have beliefs about where to go, when to go, and whether it is a safe activity. Parents who physically punish their children have beliefs about the effects of these punishments, as well as what makes a child misbehave. It is thus important to investigate these beliefs, as they form the background against which a practice must be evaluated. The *factual beliefs* that accompany the behaviors of interest represent the local knowledge that is often referred to when people are asked why they perform certain actions. As I have said earlier, these factual beliefs may be false (as those related to breastfeeding often are), or they may be true (as some related to child marriage are). Factual beliefs are part of the reasons why individuals adopt a behavior, approve of it, and reproach those who act in ways that would harm others, be they children or adults, because they may disregard what is good for them.

However, we know that interventions aimed at changing false beliefs often fail. I believe this happens for two reasons. On the one hand, there may be a failure to realize that beliefs, be they factual or normative, are part of a conceptual structure of ideas, values, beliefs, ideals, and stereotypes that help people to organize and understand the world they live in. In the next chapter, I shall discuss how beliefs may be changed, but for the moment let me point out that even simple beliefs such as "water is good for the newborn" are part of a larger set of ideas, like the division of foods, or even the mental parsing of activities into "hot" and "cold." Thus, it might be difficult to abandon any one particular belief due to its integration into a person's broader ontology.

On the other hand, conceptual structures are *shared*, so to disregard the collective nature of a group's factual beliefs would be a mistake. One may come to be individually convinced that first milk is good, but who wants to be the only one who says and does things differently? Those who may be disposed to change often face a problem of collective action, and unless individuals have confidence that the reference network, or at least part of it, will support and enact the change, the risk of suffering negative consequences looms large. This problem is present even when beliefs such as "educated women will not find a husband" are true. Here the intervention aims to help people realize that education and personal development are good things, for women and men, and that these improvements are unachievable under the current system, providing a good reason to enact change (build schools, raise the marriage age, etc.). Regardless, people who might endorse change may fear putting themselves at a disadvantage, and so refrain from action. When measuring norms in the field, we have to be aware that the factual beliefs that support them are well established (since they are shared) and thus very powerful.

## Empirical Expectations

When we observe a behavioral pattern, we want to know whether the involved parties recognize the existence of the pattern; that is, we want to know if empirical expectations exist. We should ask participants questions about specific actions they perform. For example, in the case of breastfeeding, we may inquire about first milk (colostrum), offering water to the child, stopping breastfeeding after two months, or feeding babies specific foods. We want to know what women in the community think *some, most,* or *all* new mothers do regarding each of these practices. We want to know if certain behaviors are perceived as common, normal, and generally performed within a community. We would also ask questions about the frequency of child marriage, condom use, honor killing, or open defecation. Asking these questions gives us information about the central tendency and dispersion of a collective behavior. That is, they would let us know how strong a norm is within the target population (assuming that the behavior of interest is indeed a norm). The fact that new mothers, families, or village members are widely expected to perform certain actions, however, does not tell us whether these actions are independent, as in the case of a shared custom, or interdependent, as in the case of descriptive and social norms. Similarly, such information does not tell us whether the behavior is approved of, who approves of it, and if deviations would be reprimanded or otherwise punished.

## Personal Normative Beliefs

As I mentioned at the outset of this chapter, KAP surveys only ask questions about personal attitudes. Questions may vary from "*do you think it is a good thing to do/not to do x?*" to "*do you approve of doing/not doing x?*" to "*do you like doing/not doing x?*" Answers to these questions may show a positive or negative attitude toward a specific behavior, often coupled with factual beliefs that support that attitude. The concept of attitude is rather vague, as it does not distinguish between a prudent and a moral attitude. In addition, it does not differentiate between an attitude (prudent or moral) and the warm or cold feelings one may have for a certain object or behavior, which might not be related to one's moral or prudent attitudes. I much prefer to use the concept of personal normative beliefs, with the understanding that such beliefs may also be prudential or moral. Using personal normative beliefs has the advantage of focusing attention on prudential and moral beliefs, whereas attitudes are overly broad and thus less useful in this context. However, as I have said before, knowing the personal normative beliefs of the population of interest does not tell us that a social norm exists. The only way to identify a social norm is through the mutual consistency of (incentivized) normative expectations combined with the existence of conditional preferences.

Asking about personal normative beliefs is still important, because we want to compare these beliefs with the normative expectations about what people expect *others* to think they *should* do. As previously discussed, we may come to realize that some people, maybe many, have negative personal normative beliefs toward behaviors they believe most people in their reference network strongly approve of. There are reports of situations in which only 1 percent of respondents think it is okay for a man to beat his partner, but these same respondents also believe that 50 percent of men often do, and spousal violence is indeed frequent (Parker and Makhubele 2010). These men may think that they are expected to beat their wives when they get angry or quarrel, and that they would be ridiculed if they did not. This divergence between what one would like to do and what one is expected to do may make behavioral change somewhat easier, as making private beliefs public knowledge would help the process of change.

## Normative Expectations

To verify that a socially shared normative component is present, we should check for normative expectations. There are many ways to gauge if the behavior in question is generally approved and expected, and who approves of it. For example: Is anyone telling the actors to perform or refrain from certain actions? Who would want the actors to do/not do certain things? Do actors believe most people in their reference network think they ought to behave in a certain way? What happens if someone behaves differently? Would someone punish them? Have they ever witnessed transgressions? What happened when a transgression was discovered? The purpose here is to uncover what respondents believe is approved/disapproved of by their reference network. If respondents' normative expectations are mutually consistent, we can be reasonably sure that a social norm exists.[20] There are other ways to identify normative expectations, as in the case of the third-party assessments we employ in experimental games. We could ask the actors whether they are willing to directly punish certain actions or denounce them, and how many other respondents they believe would be willing to punish or denounce. All questions about normative expectations, that is, questions about what other members of one's reference network believe should be done, punished, et cetera, should be incentivized, in order to check if the approving/disapproving/sanctioning behavior of the majority matches what the majority answers. Incentives (monetary or otherwise) motivate people to overcome any biases that might otherwise drive them to answer dishonestly, or just inaccurately.

I have repeatedly argued that normative expectations should be incentivized. This incentivization is particularly important to counteract a "social desirability bias" (Crowne and Marlowe 1960) that may be of special concern in field surveys. If a behavior is perceived as "exemplary," not only will people display a positive personal normative belief about it, but they will tend to believe that other members of their reference network feel similarly. Incentivizing accuracy should dampen the desirability bias, in that it would encourage a realistic assessment

---

20. I say "reasonably sure" because it may be the case that what is shared is an unconditionally followed and shared moral injunction, and not a social norm.

of what *most* members of one's reference network believe is acceptable/unacceptable behavior, what *most* members think people should/should not do, and so on. If these assessments are mutually consistent, we can reasonably assume that we are in the presence of a social norm (though we still have to check for conditional preferences).

To summarize: the measuring of both personal normative beliefs, empirical and normative expectations and conditional preferences is the method of choice to identify the presence of social norms. As Bicchieri, Lindemans, and Jiang (2014, 10) highlight, there must be a precise match between the content of the questions addressing personal normative beliefs and normative expectations. For example, a personal normative belief question of whether it is "good" to marry off a girl before she is eighteen would be ill-matched with a normative expectation question asking whether people in the community believe that it is a father's "duty" to marry off his daughter before she is eighteen. Because these two questions do not correspond very well, it is impossible to evaluate whether normative expectations are accurate.

The method that I propose for measuring normative expectations consists of a description of various possible available behaviors, and a request that the respondent gives his or her own personal rating of each of these behaviors. We might ask, for example, if the described behaviors are appropriate/inappropriate, good/bad, and so on. With this measure, we can calculate the most common response to each question. Respondents know that we are asking such questions to each member of their reference network, which has been clearly identified.[21] In our final step, we ask each respondent to give an

---

21. Fishbein and Ajzen (2011) offer methods to identify a reference network by asking the responders about all those who would approve/disapprove of a target behavior or about all those they may want to talk to with reference to that behavior.

assessment about the majority rating of each possible behavior we have previously described to each respondent separately. If the number of respondents is known, we may ask questions like "How many of the respondents do you think said that the described behavior is appropriate/inappropriate, good/bad, etc.?" Alternatively, we may ask questions like "What do you think a majority (most) of respondents said about the described behavior?" Even more simply (especially when employing vignettes), we may ask how respondents think a member of their group would typically interpret a particular situation. If one generates accurate responses to questions such as the ones I just mentioned, one gets a prize, thus motivating accuracy.[22]

## Conditional Preferences

After establishing that individuals have empirical and/or normative expectations about certain behaviors, we want to find out if they have conditional or unconditional preferences for acting in the expected way. In other words, do their social expectations give people a reason to act in specific ways? We want to know whether the practice of interest is independent or interdependent, and (in the latter case) whether it is a social norm.

A practice is independent if we prefer to act in a specific way regardless of what we believe others in our reference network do and/or think we should do. Our preference is *unconditional* in this sense. For instance, if parents choose to vaccinate their child irrespective of what their relatives, neighbors, and friends do, we can say they have a (socially) unconditional preference to vaccinate their child. In this case, it would be inaccurate to explain their choice by appeal to a social norm, because their

---

22. The nature of the incentive may vary. Some may receive a monetary prize, others lottery tickets for a chance of winning coveted goods or other non-monetary incentives.

choice would be the same in spite of the opinions about vaccination that may be shared in their community. On the contrary, a practice is interdependent if we prefer to act in a specific way because of what we think others in our reference network do and/or think we should do. Our preferences are *conditional* on our social expectations. Note that I am saying that a practice is interdependent *among the members of some specific reference network* that needs to be identified. To identify a reference network, we should ask questions about the people whose actions, beliefs, or preferences individuals take into account when deciding whether to perform a certain action.[23]

Individual choices might be fully explained by conditional preferences and empirical expectations, without any reference to normative expectations. Here, the person acts in a certain way because they expect others to do likewise, but not because they are expected to. For instance, if a family in India marries within their caste because they expect other families to marry within their caste, they may act because of (a) a conditional preference to marry within their caste if other families do so, and (b) the empirical expectation that other families will indeed marry within their caste. Such a family need not believe that they are normatively expected to marry within their caste in order for them to do so. They may just want to coordinate with similar families. Here, we would identify such behavior as a descriptive, but not a social norm. On the contrary, when a practice is a social norm, or is supported by a social norm, the "ought" component is prominent. Not only are individuals expected to act in a specific way, but they are also reprimanded and negatively sanctioned in a host of ways if they fail to perform. Going back to caste marriage, marrying outside of one's caste is strongly discouraged, as it would bring shame and the perception of pollution to one's family

23. This is usually done through network analysis (see Watts 2003).

and the broader caste to which one belongs. Such actions incur strong negative sanctions by one's caste: the transgressor, and possibly also his family, may be rejected from their caste and even violently punished, in an effort to avoid this frightening pollution (Fuller 1996).

Suppose we have established that a certain rule of behavior is collectively approved of and that the actors we are questioning think that most (or even all) the respondents believe it ought to be followed. Are these expectations causally relevant to the behavior we observe? Can behavior be predicted by the existence of such expectations? We must determine whether the individuals we study have a conditional preference for following the behavioral rule they know applies to their specific situation. Questions about conditional preferences must be expressed in the hypothetical mode. In experiments, we manipulate expectations by introducing different kinds of information and check for changes in behavior. In the field, we have to turn to surveys (or vignettes) that present hypothetical or counterfactual scenarios to respondents.

In hypothetical and counterfactual scenarios, we describe situations in which what people normally expect to happen has changed. We may depict scenarios in which empirical expectations are different, scenarios in which normative expectations are different, and scenarios in which one expectation is different but the others are not. In this way, we can measure the relative importance of different kinds of social expectations, which is a useful piece of information when trying to enact change. Next are examples of hypothetical questions that allow us to measure the influence of different social expectations on behavior. Would a new mother be willing to give first milk to her baby if she were to find out that (one, some, or most) other women she knows were to do it? Would she be willing to give first milk to her baby if she were to find out that nobody else will do it, but her mother-in-law thinks she should do it? What if her mother-in-law were still against giving first milk, but most other women were now giving it to their babies?

If an hypothetical change in normative expectations ("If your mother-in-law were to decide you should give your baby first milk") were sufficient to defy the empirical expectation that a specific behavior is still followed ("All other women still do not feed their babies first milk"), we would know that the normative expectation is driving behavior. In other cases, a scenario in which collective behavior is different (but normative expectations are unwavering) may elicit answers suggesting willingness to change behavior, probably because in this case the threat of punishment would no longer be credible.

Hypothetical questions are also important to determine what sort of punishment would follow norm violations, how much the threat of punishment influences norm compliance, and whether punishment is considered legitimate. Social norms often engender expectations of compliance that are felt to be reasonable, and close in a sense to "having a right" to expect certain behaviors on the part of others, who therefore are perceived as "having an obligation" to act in specific ways.

How would the respondent react if she were to observe (or were told about) behavior that is contrary to what is normally done and expected? How would others react? What if the respondent herself behaved differently? Who would disapprove? What would then happen to her? If nobody were to know that the respondent had done x, would she do it? Questions like "Is it right that someone is made to do x, even if they do not want to?," "If you knew someone who did not do x, would it be right for you to report/admonish/punish ... this person?," and "What do you think most responders who were asked this question answered?," would also be appropriate to ask in this context. Measuring normative expectations is especially valuable here since they tell us, if mutually consistent, that there is widespread agreement that certain transgressions rightfully deserve punishment. If

punishment is considered legitimate, we can infer that normative expectations are also thought to be legitimate; in this case,
many may follow a norm even if sanctions are not frequent or
even expected to occur.

As mentioned earlier, surveys that ask hypothetical questions may be difficult to answer in the field. Imagine asking a
father the hypothetical question of what he would do if he were
to realize that most of the people in his reference network have
abandoned child marriage or have become strongly opposed to
it. A likely answer from the father would be that this is not and
probably will never occur because he knows well what people
in his network do and believe. It is usually easier to answer
hypothetical questions about fictitious characters than about
real family members and friends. This is why we use vignettes.
Similar to experiments, vignettes make use of manipulations
to arrive at causal knowledge (Sorenson and Taylor 2005).
Vignettes tell short stories about imaginary characters in specific
scenarios. Asking respondents about these stories can effectively
elicit beliefs and expectations. These vignettes vary a fictitious
protagonist's social expectations (not those of the respondent)
about what people in a scenario do or what they approve or disapprove of. As Finch (1987) suggests, vignettes are particularly
useful when the questions being asked are socially sensitive and
subject to social desirability biases. Such hypothetical scenarios
provide an unthreatening and impersonal avenue for exploring
respondents' personal and social beliefs about a sensitive topic.[24]

Surveys and vignettes that present hypotheticals (or counterfactuals) can be very useful when people may have different,
conflicting motivations. I have discussed self-serving beliefs as
an example of a way to skirt a norm when other alternative

24. For further reading and examples about vignettes and how they help
    to manipulate social expectations, refer to Bicchieri, Lindemans, and
    Jiang 2014, 10–11.

norms can be appealed to. In experiments, careful manipulation of the environment allows us to introduce different norms and observe their effects on choice. In real life, what motivations win out? What would have to be different for these same motivations to lose out? Take the case of condom use. Here there may be different considerations at work. On the one hand, norms of masculinity may drive sexual behavior with multiple partners and low condom use. On the other hand, norms of responsibility toward one's family, partner, and children dictate different behavior. A man may feel the tension between the two, but in the end justify his promiscuity and condom avoidance by deciding that masculinity norms, which are shared, justified, and approved by his buddies, are more important to his identity. Surveys and vignettes may let us know how important normative expectations are in each case, whether a hypothetical change in male behavior would induce responders to change and, were we to draw attention to both norms at the same time, whether self-serving beliefs would survive the test.

## Moving Forward

Though the tools we must use in the field may differ from those in the lab, we must measure the same factors in both settings in order to accurately identify the nature of a collective practice and why people engage in it. Through surveys and vignettes, we can measure both social expectations and conditional preferences. Measuring second-order normative beliefs (normative expectations) gauges perceived consensus around the appropriateness of target behaviors and identifies the rules of behavior people share and adhere to. We can answer questions about causal relevance by checking if people have conditional preferences to engage in the practice of interest and identifying the conditions under which they may be tempted to behave differently. Asking respondents counterfactual questions or presenting them with hypothetical scenarios and vignettes is a proxy for manipulating expectations in the lab. They identify scenarios of potential norm evasion, but also tell us whether a norm has causal efficacy, and the mechanism (conditional preferences and social expectations) through which norms induce conforming behavior. Measures of consensus and conformity are crucial preconditions for designing programs to foster change. They are also useful tools for assessing if change has occurred. Norm change involves a change in social expectations, and this change can be measured through time.

Once one has identified a collective practice and investigated the conditions under which people engage in it, then an effective intervention can be devised to drive people to new, better practices. In the next chapter, I shall examine when and how a new norm may develop or an existing norm may be abandoned. In subsequent chapters, I will discuss the tools that can be used to put this change into motion, and the role of "first movers" in social change. Armed with this knowledge, an agent hoping to achieve positive social change can avoid the sort of failures that interventions have met with in the past.

# 3

# NORM CHANGE

In this chapter, I will focus on social norm change, specifically norm emergence and abandonment. I will highlight how change requires adequate reasons and how these reasons may develop. Reasons may be personal, be they factual or normative, and they may be social (i.e., social expectations). Factual and normative reasons do not stand alone: they are part of a vast web of beliefs that I will soon describe. In so doing, I will discuss the psychological mechanisms that underlie social norm change, especially the relationships among scripts, schemata, and social norms, and how change in one can lead to change in another. Since we are dealing with social norms, personal reasons may not induce behavioral change by themselves; social expectations also need to change. In what follows, I describe the relative importance of empirical and normative expectations in both norm creation and abandonment. In the next chapter, I will provide a description of the tools, both tangible and intangible, that can be employed to bring about norm change, and the hurdles one may encounter when employing those tools.

Creating, changing, and completely abandoning a social norm are all processes with similar requirements. First, there must be *shared reasons* for a change to occur. The reader may object that norms often emerge or change without any explicit collective decision, planning, or even a collective awareness that change is in fact occurring. Having reasons to enact a change may seem to involve a conscious process. But does it?

Collective behavior evolves in the direction of norm creation or abandonment, but no conscious decision needs to be involved in the process: nobody decided to start the Sexual Revolution of the '60s, or to put in place the no-smoking informal rule that eventually became legally enforced in several countries.

There are multiple factors that concur to produce such changes. The Sexual Revolution owes much to the introduction of the contraceptive pill, as well as a generational rebellion to parents' mores and the new roles that women gained in society at large. Smoking has been largely abandoned in many circles due not only to the understanding of its personal health consequences, but also to the awareness that "passive smoking" is harmful, and that the nonsmoker has a right not to be suffocated by others' fumes. Or think of mass events like the Egyptian Revolution that started in Tahrir Square in 2011. Here a "code of silence" was suddenly and unexpectedly shattered, and we are hard pressed to explain why it happened, and why it happened when it did. The widespread use of mobile phones and Internet surely fueled the movement, yet we are challenged to explain how it all started. However, if people had no reason to change, change would not occur. Had we been happy to embrace traditional sexual mores, glad to inhale other people's smoke, or to believe that a dictatorial regime was the best political arrangement we could hope for, nothing would have happened. Having reasons for change is not sufficient for change to occur, but it is a necessary prerequisite. Reasons may involve receiving new factual information, a change of personal normative beliefs, or a change in social expectations. Later, I will explain the difference between personal reasons for change and reasons for change motivated by social expectations.

Now suppose we all have good reasons to change or abandon a practice and that we are even aware of these reasons. We *know* it would be beneficial to behave differently. Yet to change behavior we must be reasonably sure we are not acting alone. The reason is simple. When behaviors are interdependent, acting alone is dicey. How strong are the negative consequences of deviating from a shared norm alone? How many must act together in order to establish a new practice? Abandoning child marriage is much riskier than starting to use soap to wash one's hands: in the first case, the daughter may not find a good husband, if she finds one at all, whereas in the second case, hand washing will be met with ridicule at worst.

Deviating from a social norm is usually much costlier, personally and socially, than deviating from a descriptive norm. Refusing to reciprocate a favor will be met with criticism, disdain, and will probably result in a bad reputation. When widely observed, such misconduct may shake the trust we have in each other, creating further social damage. Even when deviations provide social benefits, as is the case with harmful or maladaptive norms, personal costs will loom large. On the contrary, violating a convention, such as grammatical rules, will only damage the speaker, who will not be able to intelligently communicate with others. Unless this breach signals some other, more sinister intention or flaw, social blame will be absent.

As to the question about how many need to act to effect change, the size of the deviating group that is needed to yield effective change varies from practice to practice. Effective sanitation requires everyone to adopt latrines. However, when convincing families that sending young girls to school will preserve their honor, it is not necessary that all of a daughter's peers are in school—a majority will be enough. In some cases, just a small minority may be needed to change an old practice—exclusive breastfeeding, for example, can be abandoned in a small network of family and friends.

To alter or establish a collective, interdependent behavior, it is often necessary that a group coordinates on change. Coordination, in the case of descriptive norms, can be easily achieved by communication. This communication can take many forms, but it is only effective when it has reached most of the relevant reference network. In this case, it will be in our interest to follow through with the change, as not doing so will put us at a disadvantage. Coordinating on social norm abandonment is much more difficult, as I will illustrate later on. In the case of social norms, communication alone, in whatever form, even if accompanied by the common belief that others are exposed to the same message, will usually not be sufficient to generate the confidence that change is in fact occurring.

With a social norm, it is especially risky to be a "first mover" (in chapter 5 I will discuss the conditions that influence an individual likelihood to be such a first mover, i.e., a trendsetter). The behavior dictated by the norm is not just "normal"; it is also collectively approved of (or at least appears to be collectively approved of, as in the case of pluralistic ignorance). Deviating from it unilaterally invites many negative consequences. Think of child marriage. There are many reasons why one may want to marry off one's child, and many other reasons to wait until she is older, but delaying marriage in a community where all girls get married as soon as they reach puberty invites criticism, ostracism, or worse. In this scenario, late marriage harms the family and the girl. Such behavior incurs the ever-present risk of dishonor and the prospect of not finding a suitable husband. Even if one is convinced that sending the girl to school and delaying marriage would be the best course of action, one is in the grip of a *collective action problem*: it may be collectively beneficial to change behavior, but it is individually more convenient and less risky to embrace the status quo, provided one expects others to embrace it too. We conform to an inefficient or maladaptive norm because we expect others to conform as well. Mutual expectations are thus another factor that help or hinder change, because what we expect others to do influences our own choice. Remember: social norms involve interdependent actions and expectations. To escape the collective action trap, we need to develop new social expectations and trust that change is coming. So another factor necessary for transformation is a *collective change of expectations*. How this change can occur is one of the most interesting and challenging questions we have to answer if we want to understand norm dynamics. In the following chapter, I shall discuss several tools that we may use to change people's behavior as well as the dynamics of behavioral change.

Now, suppose we both have reasons to change and come to expect that most members of our reference network want change too. Still, we need to *coordinate actions* to be sure that we will end up in a better state. Expecting change is not the same as actually changing behavior, so another question we must answer is how to induce coordinated action. Behind coordinated action there are always coordinated beliefs (this is well known in game theory).[1] Coordinated beliefs simply mean that our mutual expectations are correct (i.e., what each of us expects others to do corresponds to what they actually do). However, how do we achieve such expectations? Think of conserving municipal water. People who want to be sure that their efforts and personal costs are not wasted will only reduce their own consumption when they see that enough other people reduce consumption too. In this case, public reports can help coordinate actions and expectations: by being informed that collective water consumption is steadily diminishing, one can reasonably infer that an adequate proportion of one's neighbors are actively curbing their consumption, and thus one's own conserving actions will not be in vain. In this example, had the public reports been trusted, the information they conveyed would have effectively changed (and coordinated) people's expectations, resulting in coordinated action.

1.  In order to coordinate actions, people must have correct beliefs about other people's expected behavior. In a game, if players' beliefs about each other are correct, their actions will be coordinated best replies to such beliefs (i.e., they will be in equilibrium).

Norm creation and norm abandonment thus share common features: people must face a collective action problem, they must have shared reasons to change, their social expectations must collectively change, and their actions have to be coordinated. There are, however, important differences between norm creation and norm abandonment. For a social norm to emerge, normative expectations must be created first, and empirical expectations will follow. To abandon a social norm instead, empirical expectations have to change first, and change in normative expectations will follow.

I am providing a simplified outline for what, in reality, is often a much more complex dynamic. When a social norm is abandoned, a new norm may be created, so that the interplay between the change of empirical expectations and the creation of new normative ones may happen in overlapping ways. For example, the successful campaigns for the abandonment of FGC (such as the Saleema campaign) were, at the same time, changing people's empirical expectations about the universality of the practice and creating new normative expectations about the importance of being uncut (Hadi 2006). What I wish to stress is that both social expectations (empirical and normative) will be important in norm change, but the order in which they should change will differ depending on whether we are dealing with norm creation or abandonment. We should pay attention to each type of social expectations when designing interventions.

## WHEN DO NORMS ARISE?

Sometimes a practice that starts as a purely descriptive norm comes to be imbued with meaning. Such norms may arise arbitrarily, but the behavior that gets established may take on a meaning that transcends its original function. For example, a behavior that comes to signal gender or group identity, status, or power, may become so important that members of the group may come to appreciate or even require that signal. Take tattoos, for example: to some they are merely fashionable, but for others, a tattoo could serve as an important and meaningful signal of the group or culture to which they belong (such as in the case of gangs). In a gang, refusing to get tattooed would represent an offensive rejection of the group as a whole.

Even the simple act of greeting known passersby may acquire special meaning. Simmel (1950) tells how greeting acquaintances on the street started as a simple convention, but with time acquired extra meaning: failing to greet an acquaintance eventually came to signal undesirable indifference, displeasure, or even hostility. Even something as inconsequential as table manners can become a signal of exclusive in-group membership. Norbert Elias (1978) illustrates how rules of etiquette arose as a signal of aristocratic sophistication. Thirteenth-century writings on table manners uniformly denounced "coarse" manners and promoted standards of good behavior typical of the aristocracy. Because at that time socialization mostly happened at the table, table manners became an important signal of status, demarcating a "superior" group from "inferior" ones. Good manners identified the ruling class, and uncouth behavior, coming from one of its members, signaled an offensive rejection of it. Such "uncivilized" behavior would be rebuked, as it could blur the superior group's boundaries. As illustrated in all of these examples, once a descriptive norm or even a custom has acquired an important social meaning, normative expectations are born.

Another reason why a descriptive norm, such as a convention, becomes a social norm rests on the need to eliminate negative externalities. A convention exists because it is both in the individual's and the collective's best interest to coordinate on it. The Humean convention of property, embedded in property rights, "bestows stability on the possession of those external goods, and have everyone in the peaceable enjoyment of what he may acquire by his fortune and industry" (Hume 1738, 489). In this case, what was born as a convention becomes—in my language—a social norm. Failing to create ownership rights, and a mechanism to protect them, produces a state of constant fear, conflict, and a disincentive to produce. Even those who would be tempted to steal another's property would be fearful that their own acquisitions be in constant danger. It is in each and everyone's interest to have property rights and abide by them. The reasons why a convention transforms into a social norm (as was the case in this example) should not be confused with the reasons why people try to coordinate out of collective action problems, where individual interests are in conflict with the interest of the collective.

An important reason why a social norm may emerge is to solve a collective action problem. There are two types of collective action problems, often identified as social dilemmas and tragedies of the commons. In a social dilemma, what is in the best interest of each individual makes everyone collectively worse off. Open defecation is a good example. It is a public health issue, and people are affected by their own, their neighbors', and their community's sanitation habits. The cost of open defecation or a general lack of hygiene will be felt throughout the community. Everyone benefits from the construction and use of latrines, but it is also individually rational to keep defecating in the open even when there are latrines readily available, because it is more convenient to do so. A tragedy of the commons is instead a situation in which multiple individuals, acting independently and rationally, deplete a limited, shared resource, even when it is clear that it is in no one's best interest for this to happen. Take unregulated groundwater extraction: it is in an extractor's best interest to take out as much water as possible, but multiple extractors acting in their best interests will quickly deplete the communal resource.

To solve these collective action problems, all need to co-operate with each other. Often, norms emerge to motivate such cooperation. This sort of norm emergence is what I am interested in discussing for now. History is rife with examples of norms of cooperation emerging when individuals who repeatedly interact with each other have an interest in creating and maintaining a good reputation. For example, in the market for raw diamonds, as described by Lisa Bernstein (1992), diamond traders reject the legal system in favor of an informal reputation system to regulate honorable business behavior. In Macaulay's (1963) study of the relationship between large automobile makers and their part suppliers, we see again how interactions are regulated by informal norms as opposed to by law. In both cases, the people surveyed (traders and managers) made it clear that demanding legal contracts would signal a lack of trust, and thus potentially damage a good relationship.

In addition to discussing how people can accrue reasons to want to change a damaging practice, my interest in this chapter is to briefly discuss how a new norm may not just solve a collective action problem, but also permanently change a damaging practice. An interesting example comes from my work with UNICEF: the issue of sanitation, particularly the abandonment of open defecation. Open defecation (and more generally, a lack of sanitation) is a public health issue, and its costs are felt throughout the community. There have been many unsuccessful attempts to stop it, including the building of latrines, informational campaigns, and monetary incentives. Too often the latrines were used as a stable for livestock or even as a kitchen, incentives were short-lived, and information campaigns about the damage that open defecation causes were not convincing. There are, however, some successful programs that teach about the importance of various factors to enact change, with the creation of social norms being one of them.[2]

What is common to successful programs? The first common factor is an active, collective change of factual and personal normative beliefs about the practice. It is always difficult to convince people about things they do not see: germs and bacteria are not visible to the eye, and so their consequences are hard to identify and invite a host of alternative explanations. Instead of rationally convincing individuals that particular practices are maladaptive, appealing to them on an emotional level can often be more effective. Eliciting strong emotions, like fear and disgust, can succeed at changing people's minds about some activity in lieu of reasoned arguments laced with medical data. As Valerie Curtis has extensively discussed, disgust has been successfully used as a powerful motivator of sanitation practices: "Disgust at the idea that fecal material might be present on hands was consistently reported to be the most powerful motivator of hand washing with soap after using the toilet" (2013, 97). In the case of open defecation, successful elicitation of disgust induced the necessary behavioral change.

In some such interventions, facilitators will lead groups of people through the heart of open defecation fields, effectively triggering collective feelings of disgust and embarrassment. Later the facilitators will place feces next to food, and point out how flies will flit back and forth between them, effectively simulating the disease transmission process. Through this example, food that is left out near feces is linked with feelings of disgust. The facilitator can also smear her hands with clay or charcoal, wipe them on a leaf (simulating having fecal matter on one's hands even after wiping them "clean"), and shake

---

2. The Community Approach to Total Sanitation program (CATS), promoted by UNICEF, is a successful example of a bottom-up approach where social norms were created by the target population.

hands with members of the community. The community members will get a little clay or charcoal on their hands, and consequently those who do not adequately wash their hands will be seen as disgusting.

These interventions produce a collective change in factual and personal normative beliefs toward the targeted practice. What was originally seen as benign is now seen as dirty, damaging, and dangerous. A shared sense of disgust is usually followed by a collective discussion about remedies and agreement on some form of communal action to improve the situation. Another crucial step in the creation of a social norm is thus a collective desire (and, in this case, a decision) to enact change. In the case of open defecation, people must coordinate on the building, maintenance, and use of latrines. In all the successful cases that I am aware of, the people involved in the change realized very early on that they were facing a social dilemma. It is easy to believe that if everybody uses latrines, a single person's transgression would not cause much damage. Many people may see themselves as that single person and be tempted to revert to old behavior. Due to this sort of "drop in the bucket" mentality, it is very important to implement ways to prevent mass deviance. All the communities where the practice was successfully abandoned collectively decided to sanction transgressions and closely monitored adherence to the new behavior. Children may go around with whistles drawing attention to the defectors, and elders may take long sticks, ready to "slap the wrists" of anyone who violates the new rule. In some communities fines were imposed, or admittance to traditional community ceremonies was banned. It appears that since these sanctions were collectively agreed upon, the community accepted them as legitimate, and often the very possibility of a negative sanction was enough to deter deviation. Indeed, in many communities, complete compliance was observed from the onset of the collective agreement.

Communities have developed many other creative ways of solving these collective action problems. Elinor Ostrom observed a particularly noteworthy example during her fieldwork in the Middle Hills of Nepal (Ostrom 2009). There, a small community developed a creative solution to the problem of how irrigation water should be managed. Whenever three villagers agreed that a fourth had failed to follow the irrigation rules (either by failing to maintain the irrigation system or taking too much water for himself), the offender's cow was taken into the center of the village and confined in a "cow jail." In these small communities, everyone would recognize the cow (and by extension to whom it belonged), thus calling attention to the crimes of the owner. Additionally, while the cow was in jail, anyone in the village could milk it. Much to the offending farmer's embarrassment, the cow would remain imprisoned until the farmer paid a small fee for his transgressions. What is noteworthy about this cow jail example is not just its novelty, but that the community both collectively set the rules for irrigation and agreed upon sanctions for rule-breakers. Just as in the open defecation example, the group's *collective* decision to sanction transgressions is what enabled the rules to be not only effective but also sustainable.

I want to stress that collectively deciding whether to enact sanctions helps to form normative expectations, a cornerstone of social norms. When normative expectations are in place, empirical expectations will follow, as people will observe widespread compliance with the newly established rule. When these normative expectations are developing, it seems that negative sanctions are necessary to induce people to follow a norm.[3] However, with time, the originally critical sanctions may

3. In many communities, positive sanctions were also created. Broadcasting a village's newly attained status of "open defecation free" made people feel proud of their achievement.

become less important as people internalize the norm and the new behavior becomes habitual.

We are often preoccupied with the sustainability of behavioral change, and the creation of a social norm would guarantee continuity of performance. Figure 3.1 is a basic reminder of the necessary steps that must be taken to establish a new norm. For the moment, we are only tackling the case of a norm developing from the need to stop a damaging practice and not the more complex case of a new norm emerging from the abandonment of an old one.

FIGURE 3.1 The steps taken when introducing a new norm.

Note that there is a crucial difference between descriptive and social norms with regard to emergence. As I mentioned, social norms require normative expectations, which may take time to develop. By contrast, a descriptive norm, which does not involve normative expectations, can emerge quickly, and, if coordinated behavior is achieved, it is in everybody's interest to follow the new norm. As I illustrated in chapter 1, when Sweden adopted new traffic laws, and drivers had to switch from driving on the left side of the road to the right, coordination was attained immediately. Social norms, on the other hand, always involve a strong social pressure to conform and, especially at their inception, the threat of punishment.

## NORM ABANDONMENT

It is often the case that we would like to intervene on harmful or simply inefficient norms. Similar to norm creation, norm abandonment involves several factors. One is shared reasons to change. Sometimes these reasons are already present, but there is no way to transparently communicate them. Other times, people may be completely unaware of the possibility of alternative behaviors. Even when presented with feasible alternatives, people may be convinced that their behavior is superior to possible alternatives, and consequently, they are not motivated to change their ways. Thus, a change of factual and personal normative beliefs about common practices is a necessary first step to enact change. Yet even if we may change our personal beliefs, we will not be motivated to change our behavior as long as we worry that we may be the only ones to deviate from the accepted norm. As with norm creation, a collective change of social expectations must also occur. That is, both the empirical and normative expectations that ground a social norm will also have to change. This change must be a collective one, since whenever there is a social norm, there is the possibility that transgressions will be punished. To feel safe in adopting new behaviors, individuals must come to believe that no negative sanctions will follow, which means that so many others have abandoned the old ways, that punishing them all would be ineffective or irrelevant. For even if we may come to think that many are ready to abandon a practice, we nevertheless only tend to "believe what we see."

Though normative expectations are crucial in supporting a social norm, the power of empirical expectations should never be underestimated, since they are also a pivotal component to the survival of any (social) norm, be it harmful or beneficial. In studies of corruption, it is often revealed that a large majority of people believe corruption to be bad and also believe corrupt behavior is generally condemned. Yet, as long as they believe that corrupt practices are frequent and widespread, it will be hard for people to act in ways that may be detrimental to themselves (i.e., not bribing a public officer who expects a bribe, thereby failing to receive what one should receive for free). This is a case where empirical and normative expectations diverge, and, as shown by Bicchieri and Xiao (2009), normative expectations are significantly weakened by the existence of counter-normative behaviors. Changing empirical expectations is a crucial step in abandoning a maladaptive, harmful norm.

The simple diagram presented in Figure 3.2 depicts the necessary steps that we need to undertake to abandon a (harmful) social norm. As I just mentioned, a change in empirical expectations is a crucial step, in part because it will weaken people's preexisting normative expectations. It is often the case that abandonment is accompanied by the creation of a new norm. Yet, the new normative expectations will not be sufficient to motivate behavior unless people expect the old behavior to change. The new normative expectations will act as additional motivators, supporting the behavior that people have reason to believe has changed.

FIGURE 3.2 The steps taken when abandoning a norm.

As the first step of a change in factual and personal normative beliefs requires having reasons to change them, I shall briefly highlight the challenges that we face when providing new reasons for change in both types of beliefs.

## Shared Reasons

As I mentioned, individuals must first recognize that there are problems with the current norm. Often, there are many possible and overlapping reasons for why a norm is accepted. People may not see the current norm as problematic, and even if presented with alternatives, they may defend their ways as superior. Think of gender discrimination in the workplace. In the '50s, a manager who wanted to promote women may have been perceived by his peers as odd and probably "self-interested" in a dubious way. His coworkers might not have conceived of possible reasons why a woman should be put in a top managerial position, since her place was traditionally in the family as a mother and a wife. Moreover, they might have argued that the character traits required of a manager were not typically found in women. Even when presented with alternative possibilities, men and women alike would have defended the status quo as superior. This is a typical situation where particular norms are embedded in a thick web of values, beliefs, and other norms that form shared cognitive schemata (the nature of which I will discuss later). For the moment, let me just say that the typical behavior is often not only justifiable, but it fits best with one's worldview.

A second reason why a norm may not seem problematic is the lack of knowledge of possible alternatives. In Tostan's experience with female genital cutting, the first village discussions about this practice revealed that villagers had not considered alternative ways of bringing girls into adulthood (Mackie and LeJeune 2009). Considering alternatives opens the door to discussion, evaluation, and comparisons, thereby making people more open to change.

Finally, in the case of pluralistic ignorance, individuals may not believe that the particular practice is positive or even desirable, but a lack of transparent communication and the observation that the practice is widespread makes them conclude that it is widely supported. Here, people might have good reasons to change, but they do not actively voice them. All of the above reasons, though much different from each other, are sources of resistance to discussing or changing a norm.

The interventions that are necessary in each specific case should be tailored to the nature of the reasons for compliance. In the case of pluralistic ignorance, making transparent what was obscured (i.e., what people really believe or would like to do) may lead to a sudden change in the perception of one's peers. If people are unaware of alternatives, presenting feasible alternatives may be a first step in the direction of change. Finally, in the harder case in which people value their practice, highlighting how their normative beliefs may conflict with other important values may induce them to question such practices.

For the sake of clarity, let me reiterate a distinction between beliefs along two dimensions (Table 3.1). In the following

Table 3.1

### CLASSIFICATION OF NORMATIVE/NON-NORMATIVE AND SOCIAL/NON-SOCIAL BELIEFS

|  | *Nonsocial beliefs* | *Social beliefs/ expectations* |
| --- | --- | --- |
| Non-normative beliefs | Factual beliefs | Empirical expectations |
| Normative beliefs | Personal normative beliefs | Normative expectations |

sections, I will only talk of nonsocial beliefs, be they factual or normative, and how they may change.

## Factual Beliefs

Whatever the reasons for supporting a norm, these reasons are buttressed by beliefs. Belief change is thus a crucial step in the process of norm abandonment. Beliefs may be factual: for example, people might believe that colostrum is dirty and dangerous for the newborn or that dowry costs increase with a bride's age. Factual beliefs may be true or false. The belief that colostrum is damaging to newborns is false, while the belief about dowry prices is unfortunately true. So, how can we change false beliefs? A simple, if naïve, answer is to present individuals with direct evidence that contradicts those beliefs. Those who believe that child vaccinations are dangerous should be presented with examples of healthy vaccinated children. After all, observation and direct experience are a primary way to form and change beliefs. Yet even observation is biased by preexisting beliefs that can "explain away" challenging evidence. The skeptic may have a preexisting theory of vaccination leading to, say, sterility. Even if they accept that there are indeed healthy vaccinated children out there, they may assert that these vaccinated children may eventually become sterile adults.

Yet direct observation should not be easily dismissed, at least in simple cases where alternative explanations would be difficult to harness. When the link between action and consequence is reasonably clear, observing "deviant," successful behavior may catalyze change. Showing poor Vietnamese communities that some villagers fed their children nontraditional foods (sweet potato greens, shrimps, and crabs) several times a day—and that this diet resulted in well-nourished and healthy children—led to the progressive change of traditional diets (Wishik and Van der Vynckt 1976). The link between the alternative (but still local) diet and visible benefits was direct and quite immediate.

As reported by the authors of the Positive Deviance model of behavioral change, people are unlikely to engage or believe in a practice that they have only been told is effective (Pascale, Sternin, and Sternin 2010).[4] Informing people about the efficacy of a behavior is not nearly as convincing as showing them examples of individuals who successfully practice it. As one Vietnamese villager noted after an effective Positive Deviance program (aimed at combatting child malnutrition), "A thousand hearings aren't worth one seeing" (Pascale, Sternin, and Sternin 2010, 34). Being presented with unambiguous evidence will enable factual belief change to occur more easily.

Inductive and deductive inferences, especially inferences by analogy, can serve as other ways of forming and changing beliefs (Bicchieri 1988). The weight of tradition is often due to the implicit inference that "if it has always been done, it must be good and appropriate." Testimony is another way to form and change beliefs, be it the voice of an authority or social proof. When I decide to buy a car, travel to a foreign location, or choose a hotel, I often look at what other buyers, travelers, or clients report. If a majority is satisfied, I feel comfortable with what many "testify" is good. If an authoritative medical source tells me that a medicine I take may have dangerous side effects, I will probably discontinue it because I trust the source of the information. In Islamic countries, religious leaders played an important role in the abandonment of FGC by making it both clear and public that genital cutting is not mandated by the Islamic faith.

Another reason why beliefs may be resistant to change is that those who present the new information must be trusted.

4. "Positive deviance" is a community-driven style of intervention in which alternative ("deviant") behaviors are sought out in a community. If examples of adaptive deviant behaviors are identified, they are brought to light and encouraged as an example that others can follow.

The source of the new information must be a recognized expert or a trusted authority with no obvious ulterior motives. When dealing with factual belief change, we have to be very sensitive to the source of the message and how it is presented. As a warning, though I said that the source must be credible and authoritative, even such a source may lose credibility if people disagree with the message. We need not go too far to find examples of famous scientists who risk discrediting themselves by proposing "cures" that go against what is known and accepted in medical circles. A famous example is the case of Linus Pauling, a Nobel Prize-winning chemist who, in his later years, advocated vitamin C as a cure for cancer. These claims were strongly opposed and ultimately falsified, and his status as scientific expert was consequently diminished. Authorities to whom we may go in order to spread accurate factual beliefs may be aware of the aforementioned problem, and refuse to spread our message out of fear that doing so might undermine their authority.

True factual beliefs are a very different case. The beliefs that an older girl needs a bigger dowry or that educated women have a harder time finding a good husband may be true in many communities. To change these beliefs, the facts themselves must be changed. When facts significantly change, this change may induce a big shift in people's personal normative beliefs and, eventually, social expectations. Jensen (2012) found that providing villagers with information about available jobs for girls with high school degrees and how to get these jobs led girls to remain in school a longer time, marrying much later as a consequence.

## Personal Normative Beliefs

As defined in chapter 1, personal normative beliefs are beliefs about what should be done. They may be prudential, as when we think people should not smoke because it is bad for their health. Yet the ought involved in personal normative beliefs can also be "moral," as when we say that we should treat other people fairly or that a girl ought to be married off at a young age for her own protection and happiness. Empirical evidence may help in changing prudential normative beliefs. For example, providing good schools and good jobs for girls, as well as financial incentives for families to lighten the burden of keeping girls at home longer, may change the prudential assessment of early marriage as a good insurance for a girl's future life, as there are now other safe paths to follow. But no amount of empirical evidence, per se, will change a moral normative belief. These are generally deeply held values, such as honor, purity, fairness, or justice. What usually happens is that we can change the embodiment of these values. For example, people may become convinced that honor is not necessarily best protected by female genital cutting, and that a young, whole girl is as good and honorable (and possibly even more so) than a girl who has been maimed. The Saleema campaign successfully did exactly that. Without questioning ideas of honor and purity, the campaign presented the image of an uncut girl as an image of value and integrity (Hadi 2006).

Note that changing personal normative beliefs is not strictly necessary to abandon a social norm. One may still be convinced that marriage would be the best option for young girls, but realize that the social and economic constraints have changed. Now, one observes that most girls get an education, find jobs—even husbands. As I mentioned, Jensen (2012) found that giving villagers information about the availability of jobs for girls with high school degrees and how to get those jobs prompted teenage girls to stay in school longer. Datta and Mullainathan (2012) show that parents' discovery of new economic prospects for girls led them to invest more in their daughters' education. In this example it could be the case that some parents and teenage girls cling to the normative belief that early marriage is best for girls' happiness, but since the world has changed and an educated girl can now find a suitable husband, they will conform and embrace education.

There is a certain sluggishness in personal normative beliefs of the moral kind, as opposed to prudential ones. In Figures 3.1 and 3.2, I stressed the importance of changing personal beliefs, be they factual or normative. It should be understood that a personal normative belief may include prudential as well as moral considerations. A change in personal normative beliefs does not necessarily entail a change in moral concerns—it may instead just entail a change in prudential assessments. In a generational norm shift, there will often be two sets of personal normative beliefs (of the moral kind): those of the parents and those of the children. Parents may come to adopt new prudential beliefs but still stick to the old moral ones. Younger generations, on the other hand, may be more willing to adopt new moral standards when promoting social change. When measuring personal normative beliefs, we should be able to distinguish the prudential from the moral, since the first is much more easily changed.

## AWARENESS, COHERENCE, AND BIASES

There are conditions that may help or impair factual or personal normative belief change. A condition for successful belief change is that people are aware of their beliefs. A potential stumbling block is that the new information that we want to provide may be inconsistent with the beliefs that people already hold. Another problem is that we are generally biased toward information that confirms our beliefs and thus tend to reinterpret or reject new information that is inconsistent with our worldview. Let us now consider each of these issues in turn.

## Awareness

We often wrongly assume that individuals' beliefs are at the forefront of their consciousness. Most of the time they are not. We have beliefs and can refer to them when we want to, but the majority of the time they stay dormant—exerting unconscious influence on our behavior up until the point when their validity is challenged. We often become consciously aware of our beliefs the moment something unexpected happens and those beliefs are challenged. The first time that I am attacked at night in my neighborhood, I will become acutely aware that up until that point I believed that walking at night was safe. However, this belief was not brought to conscious awareness until that point.

The same happens with social expectations, be they empirical (most other people do $x$) or normative (most other people approve or disapprove of $x$). People might not be actively aware of the normative and empirical expectations that they hold until those expectations are challenged or explicitly elicited, as when we measure them. Similarly, personal normative beliefs are not constantly at the forefront of our minds. We may become aware of how much we care for fairness only when exposed to salient, unfair outcomes. Likewise, a father may not immediately recognize that sending his daughter to school has implications for her honor and purity. Something must occur to challenge the usual conditions that keep these beliefs dormant.

Even social norms are mostly followed automatically, as default rules. In order to change norms, we have to become aware of, and consciously evaluate, our factual and personal normative beliefs, as well as the social expectations that support a norm. It is often argued that legislative interventions, educational and media campaigns, or even intensive verbal group communication are necessary tools to promote social change. One reason why they could be extremely useful is precisely that they make people aware of their beliefs and expectations, as well as the beliefs and expectations of others. I will return to this point later.

## Coherence

We tend to reject information that is incoherent with our beliefs. The more central a belief is, or the more deeply interconnected it is with related beliefs, the more difficult it is to change. Think for example of the belief in the importance of family honor: this is a core (personal) normative belief, and any intervention aimed at devaluing family honor would be doomed to failure. Honor, however, is linked to many other beliefs about men and women's roles, purity, bodily integrity, and how to maintain them, as well as how to restore honor once it has been lost. Such core beliefs, like fairness and honor, are abstract concepts, which are fundamentally tied to a constellation of specific examples and manifestations. Honor may be manifested in specific male and female behaviors, ways of acting, ways of responding to insults, ways of treating men and women, ways of dressing, ways of talking, and so on, all of which serve to inform the meaning of the original core concept of honor.

Some peripheral manifestations of particular beliefs and values may be inconsistent with other deeply held beliefs and values. For example, most parents value protecting and loving their children. Calling attention to the fact that particular practices, such as female genital cutting, may harm one's child (and are thus inconsistent with parental values) will motivate one to take action. People strive for consistency between their factual beliefs, normative beliefs, and actions (Festinger 1962), and pointing out an inconsistency will motivate them to resolve it by changing either their factual beliefs, normative beliefs, or future behavior. One of the reasons why collective discussion and deliberation may be very successful is that through discussion we are more likely to realize that there are inconsistencies in our ways of thinking and acting and come to a shared agreement about how to remedy these inconsistencies (Bicchieri and Mercier 2014).

## Biases

We tend to favor information that confirms our beliefs, especially if these beliefs are central ones. For example, in the case of beliefs about gender and race, we often treat information that is inconsistent with these beliefs as exceptions to the rule that ultimately remains unchallenged. The very successful and studious black student may be seen by some (but hopefully not all) as a wonderful exception, as much as a successful female CEO of a Fortune 500 company could be seen as an unusual, exceptional occurrence. Another way that preexisting beliefs can be maintained is by reinterpreting discrepant information so that it is no longer in conflict with our beliefs. For example, when a woman who cuts young girls received information about the potential health risks of the practice (including infection and death), her response was not irrational: she reported that of all the girls she had cut, very few fell ill, and even fewer girls died of such an illness. She provided an alternative explanation for the infections: the existence of magic.[5] Someone hated the girl and wanted her dead, and the curse worked. We should not be surprised. Even a scientist will not be motivated to abandon a well-established theory when faced with a few anomalies. In our eyes, magic is not a well-established theory, but we have

5. This was reported by a UNICEF representative from Central Africa at the Penn-UNICEF 2010 summer program on Social Norms/Social Change.

to realize that in the eyes of the cutter, it is. The mechanisms by which she assesses evidence and causality are very different from our scientific methodology but, given her criteria, her response makes sense.

Biases can reveal themselves in the way we interpret information and even laws. For example, ambiguity in the wording of a law may lead to interpretations that ultimately support the very behavior that the law was intended to combat. Consider the Myanmar Child Law prohibiting violence against children. It states that "Willfully maltreating a child, with the exception of the admonition by a parent, teacher, or a person having the right to control a child, which is for the benefit of the child" (Ko Ko 2013). Clearly, such wording is open to interpretation, so a parent who regularly beats his child could construe his violence as a "rightful admonition" that clearly benefits the child by inducing him to behave in the appropriate way. Parents will be motivated, especially when provided with such an ambiguously worded law, to interpret their arguably violent behavior as rightful and helpful to the child so as to preserve their view of themselves as good parents. Many of these biases stem from the way in which we organize and embed incoming information into a coherent cognitive system, which I will discuss in the following section.

## SCRIPTS AND SCHEMATA

I mentioned how difficult it may be to change personal beliefs, be they factual or normative. Especially when norm followers are convinced of the value of an established practice, changing their mind involves making them aware of possible inconsistencies in their belief and value systems. Our knowledge about the social and natural world is grounded in experience and structured into what are called "schemata." Such schemata are generic knowledge structures that lie at the base of our understanding of the natural and social world (Fiske and Taylor 1991; McClelland, Rumelhart, and PDP Research Group 1986; Rumelhart 1998). We have schemata for people (i.e., stereotypes), places, objects, and events. Schemata for events are called "scripts" (Shank and Abelson 1977), and these are of particular importance to social norms. Scripts are essentially prescriptive sequences of actions of varying levels of specificity that people automatically engage in (and are expected to engage in) while in particular situations. Norms are embedded into scripts because scripts contain empirical and normative expectations, and violations of scripts typically elicit negative emotions and remedial actions (Bicchieri 2006; Bicchieri and McNally 2016).

To illustrate the relationship between scripts, schemata, and social norms, consider the example of eating at a fancy restaurant. Upon entering a building of an originally ambiguous nature, one's "restaurant" schema will be activated once one recognizes that the space is filled with tables draped in white tablecloth, fancy wooden chairs that ring the tables, and people seated in the chairs with napkins in their lap, menus in their hands, or food in front of them. Once our restaurant schema is activated, and we conclude that the place is a fancy restaurant, our restaurant *script* gets simultaneously activated: we are immediately aware that certain actions are appropriate and others are not while in such an environment. We should wait to be seated, decide to eat an item that is listed on the menu, and keep our elbows off the table (assuming we have identified with the role of "customer").

Both descriptive and social norms that pertain to the restaurant experience are fundamentally grounded in the restaurant script, which is in turn triggered by the restaurant schema. There are descriptive norms about where to put the napkins, where the utensils are supposed to lie, and which hand holds the fork. We also have the normative expectation that other patrons and waiters think we should leave a tip (at least in certain countries) and treat waiters (and be treated by them) with courtesy. Various elements of a script or schema are often more central than others (e.g., "eating" is probably more central to the restaurant script than "keeping one's napkin in one's lap"), and these central elements elicit empirical and/or normative expectations that are more robust and entrenched than those linked to peripheral elements (Bicchieri and McNally 2016).

Not unlike the restaurant example, child marriage involves scripts and schemata of varying degrees of importance. There are important schemata related to gender, sexuality, patriarchy, family values, the role of women in society, concepts such as honor and purity, the nature of marriage, the idea of what a bride should be, and so on. The marriage script will vary depending on specific traditions and economic and legal conditions, and will include beliefs, values, and social expectations that stem from the schemata. The marriage script may signal that the bride should be a young, modest, virgin woman with (in some cases) a dowry that is proportional to her age, and that she will have to accept a groom who is chosen by her family.

Scripts and schemata are interconnected to varying degrees in what is known as a semantic network. The activation of one element of a semantic network will prime highly related concepts for activation. Some communities may strongly link their schema for child brides with schemata for honor and purity (as mentioned earlier), and the activation of one will prime the others for activation. This "spreading activation" can have serious implications in the case of some schemata. For example, Payne (2001) demonstrated that, when primed with an image of a black person's face, Americans are more likely to misidentify a tool as a weapon than when primed with an image of a white person's face. Payne's (2001) research illustrates how negative stereotyping caused his sample to link violence with black people in their semantic network.

Our schematic understandings of particular social groups influence what we expect from them, which behaviors we expect them to follow, and how we feel when those expectations are defied. Gender schemata, which can be especially problematic due to their typically prescriptive nature, serve as an example of how a schema can encompass both empirical and normative expectations. For example, a society may share the schematic understanding of a good wife as someone who is obedient, honest, faithful, and a good mother (as illustrated in Figure 3.3 below).

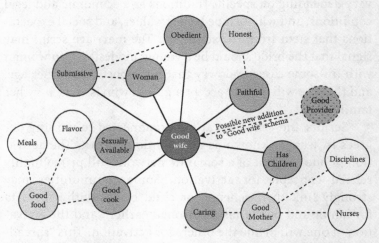

FIGURE 3.3 Possible elements of someone's schema for a "good wife" and their relations in a semantic network.

Married men who hold such a schematic understanding of a "good wife" will probably feel upset if their spouse does not conform to the idealized stereotype that they have internalized. We know that script violations elicit causal attributions: a woman who deviates from the "good wife" script with no obvious mitigating reason will be perceived as rebellious, disrespectful, and mean. The husband's expectations will have been violated, and since he perceives them as legitimate, he will respond with anger. Such a man might feel justified in beating his wife if she does not cook a good meal or provide sexual services, especially if he assumes that being "a good cook" or "sexually availabile" are central elements of the good wife schema. Punishment in this case is perceived as appropriate and possibly even as part of a husband's duties. If people collectively hold such a gender schema, its existence could serve to support and justify systematic domestic violence.

Schemata are notoriously resistant to change, as they are supported by an array of cognitive biases. For example, due to the fundamental attribution error (e.g., Jones and Harris 1967), people have an inherent propensity to infer that particular behaviors that someone engages in must be representative of the actor's personality. In the case of gender roles, if women in a society typically engage in domestic, nurturing roles, members of that society will infer that women must be fundamentally more nurturing and compliant than men. If one's peers hold similar beliefs about gender roles, then those beliefs will appear to be especially valid and will become self-fulfilling: we form expectations based on the schemata we share, act on those expectations, and interpret others' behavior accordingly. Our expectations of people can influence their behavior and subtly drive them to behave more stereotypically, thereby confirming our initial expectations (Snyder, Tanke, and Berscheid 1977; Word, Zanna, and Cooper 1974). Eventually, the belief that women are nurturing can develop into a prescriptive rule: women *should* be nurturing. The transition from the descriptive to the prescriptive occurs gradually. Empirical expectations about commonly observable behavior turn into projectable regularities in time. We come to expect certain behaviors, predict them, and infer their consequences when they are not directly observable. In this way, the script comes to be perceived as stable (Bicchieri 2006, ch. 2). A stable script tends to become a legitimate script. Those actions we regularly expect become the "right" ones, and so a normative element becomes a core part of a script. Normative expectations may be born out of regularities that we have come to consider legitimate and right.

To maintain a consistent understanding of their world, people are driven to keep schemata stable and maintain coherence in their semantic networks. One of the ways by which people maintain this consistency is inferring that ambiguous information is congruent with preexisting schemata. Encountering information that appears consistent with a preexisting schema serves to reinforce it and make it harder to change in the future. Nevertheless, despite all the forces working in defense of stable schemata, there are three ways in which scripts and schemata can change. The bookkeeping model, the conversion model, and the subtyping model represent such changes. I have discussed elsewhere (Bicchieri and McNally 2016) how these models of change relate to social norms, and I report here only some of the relevant relationships that I want to highlight.

The *bookkeeping model* asserts that schema revision will take place when people encounter an array of moderately schema-discrepant instances over an extended period of time. For example, imagine a person who originally has a schema for librarians, which features the two core elements of "quiet" and "awkward," and later gets a new job as a book salesperson. While travelling to various libraries trying to sell books, she meets librarian after librarian who are both reasonably gregarious and just as loud as the average person. Under the bookkeeping model of schema revision, the book salesperson will gradually revise the elements of "quiet" and "awkward" within her librarian schema. This model of course requires unambiguous information, for otherwise the information could be reinterpreted to be in line with the original schema.

In a recent study about what sort of variables favor or impair the abandonment of negative practices (in this case, female genital cutting), Marini and I (2016) found that, though education alone was not relevant, the presence of female teachers was highly correlated with a significant change in personal normative beliefs toward female genital cutting. According to the bookkeeping model, being exposed year after year to competent, employed female role models may change the girls' perception of what a woman is capable of and how autonomous she can be. Another example of how the bookkeeping model may work is protracted exposure to a new culture. Though child marriage is very common in Bangladesh (especially in rural areas), there is an area where it has significantly declined—Sylhet. The difference between this and other areas is that much of the Sylhet population are immigrant workers who may work in cities or abroad (Hoq 2013). Though I do not know of precise studies that measure personal normative beliefs and social expectations in this region, a reasonable hypothesis is that repeated contact with different cultures may lead to significant schema revisions.

The *conversion model* of schema change asserts that the observation of a few, highly schema-discrepant instances can induce a sudden, dramatic revision of the associated schema. It is worth noting that an extremely schema-discrepant instance is prone to being seen as an outlier or an "exception to the rule," so in order for such a dramatic instance to induce schema-revision through the conversion model, all the other qualities of the observation should conform to the original schema. For example, the people who protested in Tahrir Square in 2011 were clearly opposed to the silence that was the accepted code of conduct of citizenship. The traditional code of conduct was certainly shattered by observing this sudden spike in civil disobedience. The protesters were not different than the typical Cairo resident—they were not espousing fiery or outrageous ideas and were in every respect "normal." I suspect that many episodes of sudden and widespread rebellion are fostered by schema revision in the followers typified by the conversion model. The impact that Martin Luther King, Jr. had on attitudes toward black people and race consciousness in America may be an example of the conversion model. King was in every respect a typical middle-class black person. He was a minister, had a family, and espoused middle-class values. Being exposed to such an individual who was exemplary in some dimensions yet ordinary in others made it difficult to cast him aside as an anomaly. Thus, it became possible for white Americans to generalize King's positive qualities to black people, thereby beginning to abandon the negative stereotype that they originally held.

Finally, the *subtyping model* asserts that people accommodate schema-discrepant observations by treating them as "exceptions" and casting them into subcategories. When schema-discrepant information is subtyped, there is functionally no change to the primary schema. For example, if one had a schema for "college students" that included the element "selfish," and one observed a philosophy major handing money to a homeless person, then one might infer that college students in general are still selfish, but perhaps philosophy majors are not as bad as the rest of them. In other words, the single philosophy major was treated as an exception to the rule.

Often, schema-discrepant information threatens the way that one perceives oneself. Gender identity regulates behavior, and both men and women strive to match their stereotypical gender identity. The role-congruence that is a consequence of this motivation is an element that contributes to self-esteem. One's expectations and performance are regulated by such self-schemata, and therefore people feel motivated to cast schema-discrepant observations into a subcategory. As the literature on stereotype threat (e.g., Aronson, Quinn, and Spencer 1998; Steele and Aronson 1995) reminds us, whenever one's stereo-typical identity is made salient—and schema-discrepant infor-mation will do this—there is a tendency to conform even more to the stereotype. Subtyping may be especially common when encountering unexpected behaviors relevant to gender or race.

Whatever model of schema change may be relevant in a particular situation, there are some elements common to all three models that must be present for change to occur. First, one must encounter discrepant information (however one ulti-mately processes it). These encounters may be different behav-iors within our own group or contact with different cultures. It is also the case that the potential for change varies with the potential for disconfirmation. For example, the belief that only cut girls are honest and chaste is easily disconfirmed by the existence of uncut girls who are quite obviously honest and chaste. Crocker, Fiske, and Taylor (1984) would consider this an example of logical deniability of a schema:[6] we can easily disconfirm a schema's validity through simple observation.

Part of the success of the Saleema campaign in Sudan may be due to the fact that it induced a crucial schema change by reframing the conversation about girls' bodies (Hadi 2006). The word *saleema* means whole, intact, healthy, and perfect. It conveys the idea that being uncut is the natural, pristine state. Radio and video campaigns linked traditional values of honor

6. The term "logical deniability" is unfortunate since the authors are es-sentially referring to "empirical deniability," that is, the possibility of disconfirming a schema through observation.

and purity to the idea that uncut girls are complete and pure. Media campaigns and community discussions were framed and organized around this positive message. Perceiving girls through the "Saleema lens" functionally disconfirmed the belief that uncut girls are not chaste and pure. Prior to this campaign, the only available word for an uncut girl was *ghalfa*, which carries connotations of dishonor and promiscuity.

Other schemata are more difficult to confirm or deny through experience. For example, the belief that women are unreliable is much more difficult to disconfirm because there are a variety of behaviors that are consistent with it. Unreliability may include lying, failing to live up to a promise, being moody, or displaying inconsistent behaviors. Even if one or more of the behaviors are not present, since there are so many possible ways that unreliability can be manifested, it is very easy for such a belief to be maintained. In Crocker and colleagues' (1984) terminology, this would be an example of a *non-logically* deniable quality.

It would be wrong to think that changing a norm would invariably change the cultural schemata in which it is embedded. When I previously discussed coherence, I distinguished between core and peripheral beliefs and how certain values can be manifested in specific practices. Yet new practices can still embody these values, and we often observe the coexistence of old and new practices. For example, women may start working outside the house, yet they are still expected to fulfill all of the traditional domestic duties. An egregious example comes from interviews with men in the Nsenene village in Tanzania. These interviews highlight how the expectations of a good wife became more relaxed and came to include a new provider role with duties that went beyond household tasks, as illustrated in Figure 3.3. Yet, these new roles and activities were thought to be "additions" to a woman's traditional responsibilities. As a villager bluntly stated, "She does all the cleaning. She prepares breakfast. She works on the plantation in the morning. She prepares lunch. She goes to work on the plantation in the afternoon. She attends association meetings in the late afternoon. She comes back to make sure supper is ready. She serves supper. She goes to bed and should have sex with her husband" (Boudet et al. 2012, 38).

It appears that in many cultures, no matter what other roles women may play beyond the household, women continue to be held strictly accountable for household work and care (Boudet et al. 2012). This type of evidence suggests that certain beliefs about what can or cannot be done by a woman change more slowly than gender roles. In this case we may conclude that cultural schemata may adapt to changes in practices and beliefs that are or come to be conceived as more peripheral than the core elements of the schema. Some norms may change faster than the beliefs that are at the core of an entrenched cultural schema.

In this chapter, I have discussed how norms can change in respect to both their creation and abandonment. I paid special attention to the reasons people may have to enact change. I looked at factual and normative reasons and how such reasons are frequently integrated into a rich web of values and beliefs. Conversely, I also highlighted the kinds of biases that may stall and even prevent belief change. I stressed how norm creation involves the creation of normative expectations, whereas norm abandonment must involve the emergence of new empirical expectations that may go along with new normative ones (but not necessarily). In the next chapter, I will describe some tools that can be employed to bring about norm change. Such tools enable an individual or organization to catalyze the sort of normative change that may otherwise never occur.

# 4

# TOOLS FOR CHANGE

In this chapter, I will describe the tools that can be employed to bring about norm change and the hurdles one may encounter when employing those tools. Specifically, I will discuss the role that legal and economic interventions, the media and, on a smaller scale, deliberation play in changing personal beliefs and social expectations.

Whenever changing social norms, a crucial aspect and reason for change is a change in social expectations. Changing social expectations, however, can go from quite easy to extremely difficult. An easy case would be our realization, typically through surveys and vignettes, that the target population's personal normative beliefs about a practice are incongruent with how much they believe members of their reference network support it. Interventions that disseminate information about what people really think would replace the perceived consensus with the objective one, eliminating pluralistic ignorance. Of course, the source of the information must be credible, and the information must reach a majority of those people who still engage in that practice.

The difficult case is one in which individuals have positive beliefs about a maladaptive practice. As opposed to pluralistic ignorance, here normative expectations are correct. Not only do people personally believe the practice should be followed, but correctly believe that others also support it. Here, perceived and objective consensus coincide. Indeed, most people like and approve of the practice and are willing to penalize deviations from it. In this case, change will occur only when a change in personal reasons is combined with a change in social expectations (i.e., when a convinced individual actually observes or believes that a reasonable proportion of his reference network is changing behavior). But why would these people want to change in the first place? In the following section I discuss the possible avenues by which people may be motivated to engage in counter-normative behavior.

The literature on factual and normative belief change presents us with many ways to intervene and induce change. Educational and media campaigns, legislative and economic interventions, and intensive group communication are all ways to promote new behaviors and their advantages. Since the actions targeted for change are interdependent, a change in factual and normative beliefs must be shared by the target population. A critical quality of many of the mechanisms aimed at inducing factual and normative belief change is that they occur in a public arena, where it becomes possible for people to be aware that other people are watching or listening to the same messages. If there are avenues to discuss the messages' content, it will be possible for people to infer that others' beliefs are changing alongside their own. Remember that we are dealing with social norms. To change a norm, it is not sufficient to change individuals' factual and normative beliefs: this change must be extended to social expectations, both empirical and normative. The tools I am about to discuss, when used effectively, often perform the double function of changing individuals' perceptions of certain practices as well as their expectations about whether other people are still going to follow and/or endorse them.

## LEGAL MEANS

Legislative interventions have, among other things, a signaling function. They may signal in a public and unequivocal way that certain practices should be discontinued. A governmental diktat may easily work for conventions (such as traffic rules) because it is in the best interest of everyone to coordinate with each other, and therefore people can trust that everyone else will comply with the governmental injunction (because it is also in their best interest to do so). The law coordinates behavior via the creation of new expectations.

Legislative change is much more problematic in the case of social norms. Prima facie, it seems that a legal intervention may facilitate behavioral change by taking away the stigma associated with disobeying the norm. We would expect that enacting a law that prohibits a practice (such as FGC or child marriage) through the introduction of new sanctions would meet with success, as it would alter the costs and benefits of the targeted behavior by changing expectations and the perception of what incurs disapproval. Public opposition to the norm would become less costly, and thus we should see the targeted behavior slowly disappear. Yet plenty of prior experience (especially in developing countries) shows that change initiated in a top-down fashion, typically in the form of legislative interventions, seldom works (Stuntz 2000).

The conceptualization of legal interventions as changing the costs and benefits of a practice is too simplistic—it requires many conditions to be present in order for this solution to be effective. The question of whether laws bring about social change hinges on factors such as legitimacy, procedural fairness, and how the law is originated and enforced (Bicchieri and Mercier 2014). If we view the law as legitimate, we are more likely to comply with it. A legitimate law must ensue from a legitimate and recognized authority, and the procedures through which the authority makes decisions must also be seen as fair and appropriate. It should be clear that the law is consistently enforced and that the enforcers are perceived as honest. Anti-corruption campaigns are a telling example of ineffective legal interventions. Such laws are typically enacted during politically sensitive periods, such as in pre-electoral times or when an incumbent government wants to strengthen its grip on power (Bicchieri and Duffy 1997). A healthy skepticism would be a reasonable response to such self-serving interventions.

The opportunity to take part in the legal decision-making process, to argue and be listened to, and to have one's views taken into consideration by the authorities would all serve to motivate law abidance. It seems that trust in the legal system and the rule of law in general are important prerequisites for effective laws. Bicchieri and Marini (2016) found that, of all the considered variables, trust in formal institutions had one of the strongest correlations with abandonment of harmful practices, such as FGC, in countries where they were outlawed. In general, trust in political authorities is a crucial determinant of law abidance, as studies about the differences in legal obedience among Western European countries have shown (Fitzgerald and Wolak 2016). We may conclude that political legitimacy will result in respect for the authorities and an obligation to obey them.

However, perhaps the most important determinant of successful enforcement is a sense that the legal arrangements are not so distant from existing social norms as to lose credibility. As Stuntz (2000, 1872) incisively argued,

> If the law strays too far from the norms, the public will not respect the law, and hence will not stigmatize those who violate it. Loss of stigma means loss of the most important deterrent the criminal justice system has. If the law is to have any value at all, it needs to stick close to the norms.

For the threat of enforcement to be credible, the law should approximate popular views. The literature has many examples of laws that were successful precisely because they were sufficiently close to existing social norms. Aldashev, Chaara, Platteau, and Wahhaj (2012), Aldashev, Platteau, and Wahhaj (2011), and Platteau (2000) tell us that in Gabon and Senegal, instead of criminalizing polygamy in an attempt to encourage monogamy, the law still allowed the choice of monogamy or polygamy. In Ghana, to protect women and children's inheritance rights, a moderate law proved more effective than previous extreme laws. The moderate law makes a distinction between self-acquired and lineage property (with the latter being kept in the father's family line), thus respecting the customary distinction between the two while simultaneously pushing for better protective legislation, allowing women to keep self-acquired property. Finally, in Bogota, where high fire-arm mortality was common, Mockus, the new city mayor, decided to ban guns on holidays and, later, also weekends, sending a strong signal, but also recognizing that a moderate legal injunction would be easier to enforce and obey (Aguirre, Becerra, Mesa, and Restrepo 2005).

In support of this softer approach, Dan Kahan (2000) refers to "gentle nudges" and "harsh shoves" to point out that if a new legal norm imposes harsh penalties against an accepted social norm, police will be less likely to enforce the legal norm, prosecutors will be less likely to charge, and juries to convict, with the effect of ultimately reinforcing the social norm that was intended to be changed. Kahan argues that milder penalties are more effective and enforceable, in that they gently orient individuals toward a condemnation and eventual abandonment of the "sticky norm."

The above examples indicate that the legal approach can be an effective tool to change social expectations, but only if certain conditions are met.[1] There are extreme situations,

---

1. A legal injunction against specific behaviors may also change individuals' perceptions of the behavior. It most likely will shift one's prudential assessment of the behavior in question, but it may also influence how acceptable one thinks the behavior is.

such as in the case of dictatorships, in which conditions that would normally enable a legal intervention to be effective do not matter anymore, as people are cowed into submission by authoritarian regimes. In democratic societies, the factors just discussed must be taken into consideration when changing the law. Individuals will only be willing to abandon a standing norm if they believe that others in their reference network are changing too. Laws, however good, do not indicate that collective behavior is changing. However, they may serve the function of signaling that the old sanctions for not following a norm are losing value and, hopefully, support.

## MEDIA CAMPAIGNS

The media are popular tools for changing target behaviors. The range of technologies may include broadcast media such as radio, film and television, newspapers, billboards, internet, and even public events. Common interventions include information campaigns, edutainment (ranging from soap operas to video games), and other more modest form of collective entertainment, such as village theater. In the case of soap operas or, at a simpler and more local level, village theater, people are driven to discuss the characters and their actions. These discussions create an environment that facilitates changes in beliefs as well as in social expectations. The most successful interventions of this kind are those that feature representative characters who defy longstanding social norms and (after much drama) meet with success. Levi Paluck (2009) provides experimental evidence of such an intervention: In post-genocidal Rwanda, she randomly assigned members of twelve different communities to either listen to the radio soap *Musekewaya* (*New Dawn*)— designed to "address the mistrust, lack of communication and interaction, and trauma left by the genocide," or to a control soap (*Urunana* or *Hand-in-Hand*) that centered on themes of reproductive health. *Musekewaya* featured two representative Rwandan teenage lovers from feuding tribes (paralleling the 1994 genocide) who speak out against violence and, after a series of trials and tribulations, ultimately start a successful youth movement for peace and reconciliation. Paluck's study was effective not only at changing personal normative beliefs and normative expectations (listeners of *Musekewaya* thought that people should engage in reconciliation, and they also expected their peers to feel the same way), but it also changed their behavior. Those who listened to *Musekewaya* were significantly more likely to cooperatively share a radio that they were given at the end of the experiment (as opposed to letting its use be governed by the village leader, as was frequently done in control communities).

Effective soap operas rely on cultural schemata and scripts that people can recognize and identify with. A successful program involves suitably representative and relatable characters and events that deviate from the cultural paradigm to a sufficient degree. For example, a soap opera centered on a young girl should have her adhere to all of the values and interests that are typical of a girl from such a community (i.e., she is largely prototypical), yet at the same time she should also espouse different aspirations. Perhaps she wants to stay in school longer, marry later, or even choose her own husband. Viewing such an otherwise prototypical character has the potential to cause someone to update the associated social schemata (in this case, the schema for a "young girl").

This combination of recognizability and difference, old and new, is critical to successful media interventions. Such effective soap operas should draw upon research on script and schema change: to change people's beliefs about what they can and should expect from a particular social group, the characters should be stereotypical or prototypical enough so that subtyping is avoided, yet deviant enough so that meaningful schema revision is attained. La Ferrara, Chong, and Duryea (2012), in their investigation of the effects of telenovelas in Brazil, demonstrate how the independent female characters in televised soap operas served as behavioral role models for their viewers. In order to keep the number of characters to a manageable minimum, the older female protagonists in these shows rarely had many children, if any—a demographic quality that stood in contrast to the typical Brazilian family. They also had high divorce rates and pursued meaningful and ambitious jobs but were otherwise representative of typical Brazilian women. Once Rede Globo, the television network that broadcasted these soap operas in Brazil, introduced coverage to a new region, birth rates subsequently dropped and divorce rates rose (Chong and La Ferrara 2009; La Ferrara, Chong, and Duryea 2012). These changes were not likely due to increased television exposure, but to the lifestyle portrayed in the telenovelas: if a family gave birth to a child in an area covered by Rede Globo, there was a 33 percent chance that they would name him or her after a character in one of the telenovelas, while there was only an 8 percent chance in other regions. Interestingly, birth rates dropped the most for older women who matched the age profile of the telenovela characters. All viewers presumably updated their beliefs and expectations after watching the soap operas, yet it was the older women who found these new expectations to be more self-relevant.

Even though the characters and events in these edutainment shows are fictional, the "strong emotional involvement that the story evokes often gives the lives of the telenovela characters a central place in the everyday life of the viewers, articulating feelings [and] stimulating conversation" (Tufte 2004, 4). The characters are relatable and their plights are emotionally engaging, and thus people are driven to update their relevant social expectations and even question their existing normative beliefs. In *Twende na Wakati* (*Let's Go with the Times*), a Tanzanian radio soap opera designed to promote positive normative beliefs toward family planning practices and their adoption, there were several positive and negative role models, all of whom represented particular social groups (Rogers et al. 1999). For example, Mkwaju, a promiscuous and alcoholic truck driver (truck driving being a common occupation in Tanzania at the time), had sex with many women, stole to support his lovers, and ultimately lost his job, wife, and even life after contracting HIV/AIDS. Indeed, the many listeners of *Twende na Wakati* reported identifying with the positive role models and rejecting the negative ones. Most importantly, they developed positive beliefs toward family planning and were more likely to adopt family planning methods. The use of relatable characters and suspenseful plotlines enabled viewers to feel a genuine connection with the events that unfolded in these productions, stimulating deep and personal discussions (Slater 2002). Interestingly, changes in beliefs toward family planning were especially pronounced for individuals who reported discussing the show in addition to listening to it. Just listening to or watching these programs may have induced a shift in beliefs, but this was not sufficient to change behavior. People must be reasonably sure that their peers are experiencing the same belief shift, and discussion is one of the most effective ways to inform them that a collective change is happening.

Beyond the use of the media to tell stories that encourage societal change, informational interventions can also be effective at changing behavior simply by informing individuals of what their neighbors are doing. Schultz et al. (2007) showed experimentally that informing homeowners about how much electricity they were using in relation to other homeowners in the area led those who were above average to curb their usage and those who were below average to do the opposite. Everyone appeared to trend toward their updated empirical expectations. However, by signaling normative information in addition to this factual information (by adding a smiling emoticon next to a homeowner's electricity usage if it was below average or a frowning one if it was above average—see Figure 4.1 below for a visual representation of their finding), those who were above average continued to reduce their consumption, while those who were below average maintained their originally low energy usage. It is worth noting that Schultz et al. (2007) approach would not be effective in situations where individuals

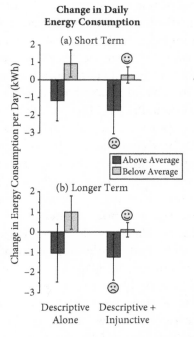

FIGURE 4.1 A visual depiction of the Schultz et al. findings. Reproduced from Schultz et al., 2007, 432.

already know how much energy is effectively used and how much people care about saving energy.

Similarly, a study by Goldstein, Cialdini, and Griskevicius (2008) shows that telling hotel guests that a majority of other guests reuse their unwashed towels prompted a large number of guests to do the same. In comparison, making an environmental (normative) appeal to save the water used in washing used towels did not have any effect. The study makes very clear the power of empirical expectations and how normative expectations, by themselves, may not induce norm-congruent behavior. Perhaps just sending a normative message may be interpreted as a sign that people usually do not conform to the desired behavior, encouraging transgressions.

Comparing a person to his peers, neighbors, or friends has proven to be an effective way to change behavior. Allcott and Mullainathan (2010) report that American households who got mailers comparing their own electricity consumption to that of their neighbors reduced their consumption as much as they would have if the cost of power had risen by 11–20 percent. Ferraro, Miranda, and Price (2011) similarly report large effects for water consumption where comparison to neighbors was much more effective than either information provision or normative messages asserting the evils of water overconsumption.

Emphasizing the percentage of people engaging in good behavior (assuming it is occurring in large numbers) may encourage those who are not yet engaging in it to join the crowd. Chaudhury, Hammer, Kremer, Muralidharan, and Rogers (2006) show that, while 25 percent of Indian teachers and 19 percent of Bangladeshi teachers are missing from school each day, between 75 percent and 81 percent show up. Where teachers have reason to believe that teachers' attendance rates are low, signaling the comparatively high attendance rates should be much more powerful than a simple message telling teachers they should improve their attendance. This normative message may give the wrong impression that many teachers are indeed absentees (if we have to tell teachers to improve their performance, then it would be reasonable for them to infer that many teachers are not behaving as they should), causing teachers to reinforce their negative expectations. Positive information about real attendance rates could be effectively disseminated through any number of media.

## ECONOMIC INCENTIVES

Traditionally, economic incentives are expected to work because they change the costs and benefits of target behaviors. For example, providing a payment for the adoption of a desirable behavior should steer individuals toward that behavior. Yet several studies have shown that monetary incentives can backfire. Titmuss (1970) showed that paying people to donate blood could result in a reduction of the proportion of donors, possibly because doing so broke a norm of voluntary contribution. This "crowding out" of intrinsic motivation is linked to a variety of signals that the monetary incentive may provide. The activity may be reframed as a monetary transaction, thus obscuring its moral significance. If the price is too low, it may signal that the activity is of low import, discouraging engagement in it. Finally, a monetary incentive may implicitly suggest that an inducement is needed, otherwise people would skirt the activity. For example, incentivizing people to pay taxes or generally contribute to a public good would signal that incentives are needed because people in general do not easily contribute.

Introducing fines may also produce a crowding out effect. Gneezy and Rustichini (2000) provide the example of an Israeli daycare that began charging late parents a small fine.

This resulted in an *increase* in the number of late pickups. Presumably, parents now perceived the monetary cost of lateness as a justification for their behavior: If they have to pay a fine, they do not feel that bad. Moreover, when one can pay a small fine for "bad behavior," it signals that the behavior was not all that bad in the first place (otherwise, why is the fine so low?). The small fine may have led people to undervalue the significance of being late, while also providing a remedy for being late (now one pays for it). When the fine was removed, parents were more likely to pick up their children late then they were before the intervention. Introducing a fine transformed what was originally a normative behavior (one should be considerate and not make daycare workers stay longer) into a market transaction, and after the fine was removed, the behavior was not restored to its original normative status.

This study and many other examples discussed in Gneezy, Meier, and Rey-Biel's (2011) paper show the dark side of the crowding out effect of monetary incentives: when the incentive is removed, the motivation to perform a task without the additional monetary incentive can be permanently reduced. The crowding out effect is an example of involuntary framing of a situation through the activation of a particular script. A monetary incentive may activate a market script, making admissible the previously disapproved activity (so long as a price is paid). What was originally a normative script is transformed into a market transaction.

Another effect of pricing an activity (such as providing incentives for pro-social behavior) is that the activity gets anchored to a specific monetary value that might be much less than what one would have originally valued it at. Engaging in pro-social behavior, such as volunteering, may gratify people, yet paying them a small fee to volunteer may downgrade the activity by signaling that it has little value. Gneezy and Rustichini (2000) suggest that the opposite can be achieved by significantly increasing the price paid for an activity. The short-run "price effect" thus produced will make people value the activity more than they originally had.

In addition to changing normative behaviors into market transactions, another negative effect of monetary incentives is that they signal, both to one's peers and to oneself, that one is "doing it for the money" rather than for good moral reasons. Mellström and Johannesson (2008) show that simply offering a small monetary incentive to donate significantly decreases blood donation rates, but when people are offered the opportunity to donate the money to charity, blood donation rates return to their original level. Donating the money to charity reaffirms the original signal that one is morally motivated.

Monetary incentives have been used to build latrines, send girls to school, curb child marriage, encourage the use of condoms, and get children vaccinated. The results of such incentives are mixed. Incentives at work in education have often been successful. Paying families to keep girls in schools longer increases the opportunity cost of marrying them off earlier, and makes the girl more valuable to the family, who begins to treat her as a long-term investment. Not only are girls kept in school longer, but they are better nourished as well (Jensen 2012). In this case, the incentive is very specific (keeping the girl in school for a set number of years), the target behavior is limited in time, as school eventually ends, and it is easy to monitor successful outcomes. Incentives to build and use latrines, however, have not met with much success. Latrines are initially built, but soon are put to other uses (as storage, kitchens, or animal shelter).

The monetary incentive in this case was meant to induce a bundle of different activities, since abandoning open defecation involves not just building latrines, but also keeping them functional, and using them consistently. Monitoring all such activities is difficult. Moreover, the target behavior is not limited in time, but has to continue indefinitely. The World Bank Water and Sanitation Program in India has provided significant amounts of money for constructing latrines. Yet, even with significant subsidies to induce people to use them, half the toilets went unused (Sanan and Moulik 2007).

One reason the program did not work was that the target community was not involved in a process of understanding the damage caused by open defecation, which could have resulted in a collective decision to abandon the practice. What is needed to abandon open defecation is a different sort of incentive; people will have to be convinced that the sustained and continuous effort is worthwhile. The norm formation model I have described (see chapter 3) suggests that, when dealing with ongoing, long-term practices that involve many connected behaviors and considerable monitoring, sustainable behavioral change requires a paradigm shift from economic incentives to the establishment of new norms.

## DELIBERATION

Community deliberation is often touted as an effective tool for changing maladaptive practices. The social norms we may come to discuss in collective deliberation are part of a rich web of beliefs, values, and scripts. Deliberation unearths such beliefs, values, and their connections. When deliberating, we may become aware of inconsistencies between our own beliefs or between our beliefs and the new information. For example, realizing that female genital cutting could result in bodily harm would make one also realize that continuing to practice it would be in conflict with beliefs about protecting the health and life of one's children. We may also come to realize that some of the premises that we accept must lead to some logical conclusions that, in fact, we normally reject (Mercier and Sperber 2011). For example, if we believe that men and women are equal, we cannot consistently maintain that sons should be favored over daughters. Discussions are one of the best ways to unearth such inconsistencies. After identifying inconsistencies, people are strongly motivated to alleviate them, eliminating the dissonance between beliefs that do not fit together (Mercier and Sperber 2011). As I mentioned, people will not attempt to address conflicting beliefs on their own. In order to change, people must have reasons to do so, and since we are dealing with social norms, the reasons for change must also be shared. Deliberation, when conducted under appropriate conditions, is often a powerful tool to foster collective reasons for change.

Deliberation creates an environment for people to speak about topics that are otherwise social taboos. It is often argued that a great advantage of deliberation is the lifting of pluralistic ignorance—where people follow a norm because they believe that it is supported by the majority of the population, even if their belief is mistaken. Yet, if a friendly chat were sufficient to solve the problem, we would see a quick disappearance of maladaptive norms that are not endorsed by the majority of the population. Exposing people to their group's beliefs and making them realize that many others share their doubts about a common practice will come to naught unless they are presented with a superior, feasible alternative. Moreover, even if alternatives are presented and a collective agreement is reached that one of them is indeed superior, changing factual and normative beliefs may not necessarily lead to a change in social expectations.

Deliberation in small groups runs several risks. One is polarization: often participants with similar ideas will radicalize (instead of moderate) their viewpoints, as studies of civil juries show (Myers and Kaplan 1976). One remedy would be to introduce some measure of diversity into the discussing group. In many experiences of deliberation promoted by UNICEF and NGOs, the group is not restricted to the population at risk (e.g., women), but is inclusive of all the members of the reference network of the targeted subpopulation. This may include men, relatives, extended families, religious leaders, village leaders, and others.

For deliberation to be productive, discussion should be sincere and unrestrained, and people should feel free to openly express their opinions. One of the factors that can derail such effective deliberation is the existence of power dynamics. For example, when some discussion participants are in a more powerful position than others, the less powerful might not feel free to argue against the points brought up by the more powerful. This situation often occurs in discussions between men and women, especially in cultures where women are not accustomed to expressing their opinions. Many of the external factors that can hamper the effectiveness of a discussion can be greatly alleviated by having an unbiased facilitator guide the discussion. One of her duties will be making sure that everyone has a chance to speak and is respectfully listened to. She can also give underrepresented viewpoints a voice.

Discussion can also be derailed by internal hurdles. A common barrier to a candid discussion is the existence of norms that dictate how we should talk about norms. Mackie and LeJeune (2009) report that the mere mention of FGC would be a serious normative breach in some groups. Forcing people to talk about taboo topics will backfire. Bicchieri and Mercier (2014) discuss how, if criticism of the practice is not allowed, a false impression of consensus can strengthen pluralistic ignorance, and give the practice stronger legitimacy. In these cases, too, an external agent may help direct the discussion in a more productive fashion. Respected leaders (be they religious or secular), for example, may help people realize that some of their normative beliefs are unfounded.

Regardless of the facilitator, there is a risk that those who offer an argument that unearths the inconsistency in a listener's beliefs may be perceived to have a personal agenda, and thus appear manipulative. If the issue being discussed is emotionally loaded, as is often the case when discussing core values and especially in cases of moral dumbfounding, where people have strong moral reactions but fail to establish any kind of principle to explain their reactions, arguing about the issue may prompt the listeners to stonewall the argument. In many cases of successful deliberations, such as Tostan in Senegal, KMG in Ethiopia, and IHRE in India, core values of family, honor, and the importance of marriage were purposefully never challenged (Bajaj 2011).

Discussions can explicitly show the reasons why a practice is inconsistent with some core beliefs that we hold. They can also slowly lead the participants to realize on their own that some of their beliefs are in conflict. Gillespie and Melching (2010) describe in great detail how Tostan uses implicit arguments to let people decide on their own whether to abandon maladaptive practices. Many of the successful interventions that use community deliberation share a *maieutic*[2] character of guiding people to reach their own conclusions from shared accepted premises. We should recall that social norms are not isolated cultural practices: they are steeped in a complex network of factual beliefs, normative beliefs, and values. We know that some are more central than others and that certain links in a semantic network are stronger than others. For example, the belief in the importance of honor is likely more central than the belief that a girl should be meek and obedient. A rebellious girl can always be disciplined to protect family honor. Purity, however, is strongly connected to honor. If the girl were to tarnish

---

2. This is the way Socrates led his disciples to unearth inconsistencies and come to correct conclusions.

her family's honor through pre-marital sex, that honor may be permanently stained. Because of different strengths in the links within a semantic network (purity is more strongly linked to honor than meekness), a good, productive, and protracted discussion should never be focused on just a single practice or norm that the discussants have adopted. Ignoring the connections between certain practices and the web of beliefs they are embedded in could prevent the recognition of inconsistencies between these elements.

Implicitly directed arguments, which allow participants to discover inconsistencies on their own, would encourage a discussion of a broader array of elements more than explicitly directed arguments (which directly expose inconsistencies). They may highlight the importance of certain values and core beliefs without immediately involving a discussion of more peripheral beliefs and practices. In Tostan's work, the community argues about the importance of core values, such as respect for human life or love for one's children. Discussants work out, in a process of collective deliberation, the practical consequences of these core beliefs and values. Coupled with credible factual information about certain practices, individuals may come to realize that what they do contradicts what they *should* do as mandated by their values and commitments (Diop et al. 2004).

Another important consequence of deliberation is the potential severing of weak links in a semantic network. In a semantic network centered on FGC, honor may be strongly linked to purity and purity weakly linked to FGC. It would be easier to sever the link between purity and FGC than to sever the link between honor and purity, since the link between purity and FGC is not central to numerous other beliefs. Severing weak links becomes easier when alternatives are presented (a girl can still be pure without being cut). In this sense, central values and core beliefs are not challenged, but individuals are reoriented to draw different conclusions. The Saleema campaign accomplishes this reorientation by acknowledging that core values such as honor and purity can be better embodied in a whole, uncut, and untouched girl's body.

I have argued that individuals need reasons to change their beliefs and behavior. People are not likely to engage in spontaneous discussion about the validity of norms or practices that have been in place for a long time. Moreover, drawing attention to implicit core values and their consequences as well as potential inconsistencies between those values and certain practices is not a short-term, easy process. This is another reason why discussions should be guided. Facilitators who know and share certain core values and beliefs (and thus are likely to be accepted by the community) play an important role in steering the discussion down a particular direction such that implicit core values are unearthed, and inconsistencies are highlighted.[3] Good, guided discussion makes it possible to successfully reorient particular schemata within the group's semantic network.

Group discussion has an important public dimension. During these discussions, people's acceptance of certain arguments becomes visible, which may induce participants to be more willing to accept such arguments themselves. Discussion helps to change our personal normative and factual beliefs and to observe that others' beliefs are changing, too. The process of belief change becomes a collective one, as we change our minds together. Collectively changing personal normative beliefs weakens the normative expectations that support the challenged norm, at least within the group of discussants. Yet, accepting an argument and changing behavior are very different things. Group discussion may successfully change personal normative beliefs, even "local" normative expectations, but

3. There are many examples provided by UNICEF and NGOs of attempts (some more successful than others) to direct group discussions in intervention settings.

what leads to stable behavioral change? For a norm to change in a large population, a sizeable consensus must be reached. In rounds of collective discussions, a group may come to agree that the old norm should not be upheld and subsequently envision and agree upon a new practice and promise to follow it (Haile 2004). Unless the group is isolated and interactions with other groups are limited, the problem of moving a large majority in a counter-normative direction remains a difficult one.

Often, the tools for change that I have discussed are implemented in isolation from each other, and I do not think this is a good idea. Each one, if used well, will have a cumulative effect on the others. Media campaigns should accompany new laws and perhaps economic incentives. All these interventions endorse new practices, informing people about good, feasible alternatives. The attempt that media campaigns make to change some entrenched schemata will be amplified when accompanied by effective and appropriate grassroots discussions.

Even in the best possible circumstances, when several tools are employed simultaneously to change collective beliefs, behavioral change may be difficult to attain. People will need to be reasonably sure that behavior is effectively changing and, thus, that they are no longer violating the previously accepted norm. In the next chapter, I explore how behavioral change is often spearheaded by trendsetters, or "first movers," and the sort of characteristics they may possess. Trendsetters may be individuals, small groups, or even the media. In each case, these agents initiate change, serve the critical role of signaling that change is indeed occurring, and help to coordinate behavioral change on a broader level.

# 5

# TRENDSETTERS

We know that belief change in isolation may not lead to behavioral change. Even if our personal normative beliefs and
normative expectations are undergoing change, we need to
be reasonably sure that we will not find ourselves in a minority by behaving differently. This is typical of collective action
problems, where we all have reason to think that a new practice
would be better for us, but most individuals hesitate to change
for fear of incurring a cost. What kind of first mover would be
willing to incur this cost, and how can they be identified?

Before moving on to a more detailed examination of trendsetters, or "first movers," I will introduce the concept with an
example from history. In the early 1960s at the onset of the Civil
Rights Movement, black Americans had ample reasons to protest the systemic inequality in the United States (again, reasons
for change are a prerequisite for the collective change of social
norms), but many likely felt uneasy about protesting without
others to back them up. Andrews and Biggs (2006) analyze the
forces that contributed to the rise of sit-ins (a vehicle for protest) and highlight the types of trendsetters who marshaled the
movement into full force.

The more autonomous[1] and affluent black adults and black
college students there were in a city, the more likely the city was

1. In Andrews and Biggs' study, autonomy in a black community was inversely measured by "the percentage of male labor force relegated to un-
skilled occupations—servants and laborers" (2006, 760). Later in this
chapter, I provide more fine-tuned psychological measures of autonomy.

to experience sit-ins. Autonomous black adult populations had a greater capacity to dissent, and black college students likely perceived dissent to be less risky. Black students probably held this perception since fewer social sanctions could be applied to them: they could not be fired from a job for staging a sit-in the same way that a working black adult could be.[2] The very nature of autonomy suggests that autonomous individuals will be more prone to deviate from maladaptive practices. I will discuss the relationship between autonomy and dissent in greater detail later on.

Even if trendsetters deviate from an established practice, they will never influence their peers if news of their deviance does not spread. Thus, it is not surprising that, in Andrews and Biggs' (2006) analysis, news coverage had a particularly pronounced impact on subsequent nearby sit-ins. Such coverage reliably signaled that dissent was both possible and already occurring. Communication within social networks had a similar yet diminished effect, as these networks could not facilitate the spread of information to as many people or as many locations as the radio or newspapers could.

Though there were several sit-ins that occurred prior to 1960, they all failed to spark the same social fever that the one in Greensboro, North Carolina, elicited. Andrews and Biggs hypothesized that this was the case for two reasons: first, the black college student population increased 35 percent over the course of the 1950s, so by the time 1960 hit, there were many more individuals who felt free to publically dissent. Second, newspapers were less likely to report such behavior prior to the 1960s, so information dissemination was much less likely to occur. The failure of previous movements to spark social change shows that even if there are trendsetters presently

---

2. Certainly, students could be expelled from college, but expulsion is not as dire a threat as losing the ability to support one's family (which would be the case if one lost one's job).

acting against established practices, their deviance will not necessarily influence their peers. Their behavior (if well publicized) merely increases the likelihood that others will follow.

Certainly, as Andrews and Biggs' (2006) analysis highlights, trendsetters are important catalysts of social change, but what are the makings of a trendsetter? In a social environment in which only a small proportion of individuals are willing to first deviate from an established norm, those individuals should have considerable reasons for deviating, they should be less sensitive to the norm in question, and they should have diminished perceived risks of deviating. I have already discussed many of the possible ways by which people can develop reasons to deviate and why it is important for these reasons to be shared, so let us focus now on how to assess people's sensitivity to a norm.

## Norm Sensitivity

Sensitivity to a norm refers to how much a person adheres to what the norm stands for (Bicchieri 2006, 52). Norm sensitivity embodies one's personal reasons for adhering to the norm. A highly sensitive individual could list several good, important reasons why a particular norm should be enforced, whereas an individual with low sensitivity, who does not care much about what the norm stands for, may only list the fact that, since the norm is widespread, it makes sense for her to obey it (to avoid the sanctions that transgressions incur). Let us call a person's sensitivity to a particular norm, n, $k_n$. For example, a person who is not very convinced of the advisability of child marriage will have very low sensitivity to that norm (in other words, a very low $k_n$), whereas a person who is convinced that child marriage is the best way to protect a child's honor will be highly sensitive to such a norm. Both individuals, however, may be highly sensitive to a norm of reciprocity. In these respects, norm sensitivity is highly domain specific. A person may have a disposition to be less sensitive to certain norms for various reasons that go beyond the scope of this chapter.

Sensitivity to a norm may be subject to change when a person receives information showing how harmful a certain practice might be. For example, an avid recycler may discover that recycling actually pollutes the environment and thus start questioning the practice. A construction worker may come to realize that not wearing a protective helmet may leave him vulnerable to falling debris, even if wearing helmets is touted as "un-masculine" in his group.[3] In these cases, new information may change an individual's sensitivity to a norm, yet, unless one is willing to break from tradition, this low sensitivity will remain a necessary, but not sufficient, condition for change. In chapter 2, I discussed how to assess the presence of conditional preferences. Having conditional preferences implies that, in the presence of the right social expectations, a person would follow a norm. Vignettes, in particular, help us measure how much a behavior would change in response to a change in expectations or information conditions. Measuring how much, or how fast behavior could change provides us with a rough measure of individual sensitivity to a specific norm.

We might assume that the $k_n$ are normally distributed,[4] but this may not be the case when the norm is socially important and has been in place for a long time. In this case, the distribution

3. I owe this example to Javier Guillot, who, when consulting with a large construction company in Colombia that had an excess of accidents, realized that workers did not want to wear helmets for fear of being perceived as "sissies" by their co-workers.

4. A normal distribution, which people will recognize by its bell-shaped curve, is a statistical distribution of elements (personalities, height, blood pressure, etc.) where most of these elements fall close to an average. Fewer and fewer of these elements fall farther and farther from the average. For example, if the variable of interest were height, and the average were 5'10", then most people would have a height close to the average, and fewer and fewer would be increasingly taller and shorter than the average.

of $k_n$ will be skewed, in that most of the population will be very sensitive to it, and only a small, thin tail of individuals will not care much about it. With a new or less important norm, the distribution may again not be normal, in that most people may have low to moderate sensitivity to the norm, and it would therefore in principle be easier to shake adherence to it.

## Autonomy

Individuals who are willing to break from tradition, beyond a low level of sensitivity to a particular norm, should also be relatively insensitive to general pressures of conformity and be autonomous in their decision-making. Unfortunately, to identify such individuals, one must overcome the hurdles of defining and operationalizing autonomy. There are many philosophical and psychological definitions of autonomy, and only the psychological ones have been operationalized (and are thus useful when attempting to identify potential trendsetters). Yet, even these operational definitions of autonomy are not all predictive of the same kind of trendsetter.

One primary distinction that has been made between two different forms of autonomy is "reactive" and "reflective" autonomy, or the distinction between the "freedom from the governance of others" and the "freedom to self-govern," respectively (Koestner and Losier 1996, 471). Many of the proposed ways to measure autonomy tend to tap into one of these two definitions (Hmel and Pincus 2002). Measurements that tap into reactive autonomy assess an "independent form of autonomy, manifested in agency and interpersonal separation," while measurements that tap into reflective autonomy represent an "interdependent form of autonomy, strongly and positively interpersonal in nature" (Hmel and Pincus 2002, 305). The two forms of autonomy are only loosely associated in individuals (Hmel and Pincus 2002; Koestner and Losier 1996). Individuals who score high on measurements of reflective autonomy tend to be extroverted, assertive, altruistic, open to new values, and enjoy playing with ideas and solving puzzles, while individuals who score high on reactive autonomy tend to be disagreeable and introverted (albeit assertive).[5]

Theoretically, it is reasonable to imagine that people who score high on reflective autonomy (who tend to be independently motivated yet positively interpersonal) are more likely to be central in a particular social network, while the people who score high on reactive autonomy (who tend to be independent and solitary) are more likely to be peripheral members of their social network. Both types of people should be agentic and (theoretically) willing to deviate from customary behaviors if given adequate reasons for doing so. However, people would be more likely influenced by the actions of reflectively autonomous agents: if they are indeed central in their social network, then their actions would be more readily observable, and their likable personalities would make people more willing to listen to and follow them. That said, these likely more central and autonomous individuals would also be subject to a greater number of potential social sanctions than socially peripheral and autonomous individuals would be.[6]

Research using the Index of Autonomous Functioning (Weinstein, Przybylski, and Ryan 2012), a measurement that taps into reflective autonomy, highlights the paradox of being

5. As measured by the NEO-PI-R (the Revised Neuroticism-Extraversion-Openness Personality Inventory). See Hmel and Pincus (2002) for further information on the personalities that tend to be associated with these two manifestations of autonomy.

6. It should be noted that often people who are at the center of a network and occupy a leading position are prototypical, in the sense that they embody the norms and traditions of their community. Even so, a central and very reflectively autonomous individual may not feel the same drive to be culturally prototypical that another central yet less autonomous individual would.

autonomous and yet central in a social network. Individuals who score high on this inventory appear to care about their neighbors in addition to generally being autonomous. In a collaborative laboratory task, such individuals were more likely to sit close to fellow subjects (a behavioral proxy for feelings of closeness) and to report having greater empathy, feelings of closeness to their partner, and autonomous motivations (Weinstein, Przybylski, and Ryan 2012). Despite being "self-driven," they appear to have a greater propensity to care about their peers. If given adequate reasons to abandon a practice, it is reasonable to expect that individuals who score high on this index will use the information, become less sensitive to a norm that they now perceive as harmful, and be more willing to change the practice for the benefit of the group they care about. Yet, as we shall see later on, their perception of the risks of deviating from a social norm will still loom large in their decision-making.

An example of a reflectively autonomous agent is the wife of a village leader who, after being convinced of the merits of exclusive breastfeeding, decided to publically reject feeding her newborn water in favor of breastfeeding.[7] Here, the leader's wife was autonomous in that she was sufficiently uninfluenced by the pressures of conformity to feed her child water and not colostrum, and was reflectively so because she deviated in part for the benefit of her peers. In addition, she was in a position of power, so she knew her behavior would be especially scrutinized by other villagers, but also possibly used as a model for their own behavior. Indeed, after the villagers saw how her child did not become sick (as they had anticipated), they began to reconsider early breast milk as a viable food for newborns. However, it is important to acknowledge that her being in a position of power and at the center of a network made her actions

7.   As reported by Felicite Tchibindad.

much more visible and more subject (in principle) to potential sanctions, but her position also mitigated the risks of criticism.

Regardless of the particular manifestation of autonomy, there is much evidence that autonomous individuals have a sense of agency and freedom from the control of others. Research using self-determination theory's operationalization of autonomy (being internally, as opposed to externally influenced) found that autonomous college males were much less sensitive to social pressures when determining whether to consume alcohol and how much to consume (Knee and Neighbors 2002). Having a "controlled orientation" (the opposite of an autonomous orientation; Deci and Ryan 1985) predicted whether male students would have extrinsic reasons to drink, which, in turn, predicted perceived peer pressure and drinking behavior. Similarly, adolescents who reported having greater needs for autonomy were less susceptible to social pressures to smoke (Hill 1971), despite the fact that the influence of peer pressure increases in adolescence (Krosnick and Judd 1982).

When deciding whether to deviate from an interdependent collective practice, it is the same individuals who are capable of resisting pressures to drink or to smoke (and more generally break from their crowd) who will be able to resist normative control.[8] Indeed, in Andrews and Biggs' (2006) research, the presence of autonomous black adults in a city predicted a sit-in. In theory, scoring high on either reflective or reactive autonomy should make people less sensitive to normative pressures, but network centrality should theoretically increase the risk of the negative sanctions that one incurs when deviating

8. Autonomy is also malleable: Offering extrinsic pressures (deadlines, bonuses for performance) decreases intrinsic (autonomous) motivations (Amabile, DeJong, and Lepper 1976; Deci 1971), and some career or life choices are certainly more conducive to autonomous functioning than others.

(the more central one is, the greater number of possibly disapproving peers one knows).[9] Though the reflective autonomous individuals (who tend to be more agreeable and gregarious) may be more likely to be observed by (and thus influence) other people, their increased visibility also makes their deviance more risky. In this respect, it is the reactive autonomous and less central individuals who will be more likely to deviate on their own. Indeed, Kadushin (2012) points out how trendsetters are more likely to be fringe members of society. That said, this fringe behavior will not have much influence until it is adopted by more central and integrated members of society (i.e., "opinion leaders" [Kadushin 2012, 143]).

## Perceived Self-Efficacy

In addition to autonomy, one's perceived self-efficacy should theoretically contribute to one's likelihood to abandon a norm. Perceived self-efficacy, a concept that is similar to, yet independent from autonomy, is the perceived capacity to exercise control over oneself and the events in one's life (Bandura 1993). Perceived self-efficacy is distinct from autonomy in that autonomy is typically defined[10] as one's perceived ability to act independently from others' control, while perceived self-efficacy focuses on how much *influence* one feels one can exert with one's actions. Theoretically, trendsetters should be both autonomous and have high perceived self-efficacy before being willing to deviate from an established norm. When dealing with counter-normative actions, one must believe that one's actions

9. The case may be different for powerful people who could, to a point, be subject to fewer sanctions for a variety of reasons. One reason may be the fear of retaliation that the powerful can exact on the less powerful.
10. Though again, definitions vary.

will carry weight and lead to some personal benefit (especially if one is reactively autonomous) or some broader societal change (especially if one is reflectively autonomous) before being willing to engage in them.

## Risk Sensitivity and Perception

Perceptions of risk also determine whether someone is willing to be a first mover. Prior to the Civil Rights Movement, staging a sit-in was a highly risky activity, and indeed it was the presence of black students in a city (for whom deviating incurred fewer risks than for working adults) that predicted the incidence of a sit-in (Andrews and Biggs 2006). For black Americans, the risk of deviance was very real, but the perceived magnitude of such risk is what ultimately influenced their behavior. Students who perceived the risks to be smaller than they actually were or who were generally risk-seeking would theoretically be more likely to stage a sit-in than risk-averse students or students for whom risks loomed large. In this example and in many others, the risks of being a first mover are especially high, so trendsetters are likely to be either particularly risk-insensitive or misperceive the actual risks of deviance. In what follows, I will distinguish between risk sensitivity and risk perception, and provide a parameter that takes both into account in determining one's willingness to act.

Psychological research on risk sensitivity sheds light on how it influences behavior and what types of people tend to be risk-seeking or risk-averse on a general level.[11] Risk perceptions,

---

11. In studies investigating the typical personality of risk takers, Fenton-O'Creevy, Soane, and Willman (2001; see also Nicholson, Soane, Fenton-O'Creevy, and Willman 2005) found that they tended to score high on extroversion and openness to experience and low on conscientiousness, neuroticism, and agreeableness. These characteristics would help in identifying risk-taking personalities.

on the other hand, vary significantly according to the specific situation. In a study of adolescent alcohol consumption, perceptions of the risks and benefits of alcohol-related activities were highly predictive of adolescents' willingness to participate in them (Hampson, Severson, Burns, Slovic, and Fisher 2001). Perceptions of risk varied considerably in the sample, but were always present (at least to some degree). Real and perceived risks interact in their influence on behavior: ultimately individuals' perceptions of risk matter to their choices, but they would not likely perceive risks if risks did not exist in the first place. However, even when dealing with very real risks, interpersonal differences mediate their strength.

I should stress again that a person's risk sensitivity is invariant, but risk perception may vary across situations. Risk sensitivity is a stable disposition. It is often assumed that criminals, adolescents with ADHD, and entrepreneurs share a low sensitivity to risk. They largely discount the future or have permanent, overly optimistic views of their chances of success. Risk perception, on the contrary, will depend on the situation, what is at stake, and the action under consideration. The same person could have high or moderate risk sensitivity but a very low risk perception in a particular situation. For example, a person of moderate risk sensitivity would not dare cut in line at a supermarket because of the likely disapproval that this action would incur, but the same person may feel less restrained stealing some minor item in an unpopulated aisle. In other words, this person has moderate risk sensitivity, but her risk perceptions vary across situations.[12]

Risk perception varies in the same person from domain to domain, and if we limit our consideration to a particular domain (such as cutting in line), risk perception will also vary

---

12. Other elements such as optimism and pessimism, which I will not discuss here, may influence one's propensity to perceive high or low levels of risk.

across individuals. One individual may optimistically believe that cutting in line would, at most, induce a sneer from other customers, whereas another individual may imagine that the same action would induce insulting and embarrassing comments. In what follows, I will use a variable, $\breve{\alpha}$, which is a function of $\alpha$ and $\alpha_n$, where $\alpha$ represents an individual's risk sensitivity, a stable disposition, and $\alpha_n$ represents that individual's risk perception relative to a particular domain or, in our case, a particular social norm ($n$). Risk perception may depend on one's uncertainty about the objective risk incurred in deviating from a social norm. It may also depend on the degree of optimism about the success of one's actions (which in turn may be related to perceived self-efficacy), or it may be related to the tradeoff between the risk of negative sanctions and the much larger benefit incurred in initiating new behavior (focusing on expected benefits may "dampen" risk perception). There may be many reasons why someone may have low perceptions of risk in a particular situation. What matters is that people will have different thresholds for action based not only on their personal allegiance to a norm ($k_n$) but also on $\breve{\alpha}$, which includes both their risk sensitivity and their particular risk perception in that situation.

The behavior of trendsetters points to the possibility of abandoning a social norm. This signal diminishes the perceived risk of further deviance for people who have higher $\breve{\alpha}$, and enables those decision-makers to follow suit. I assume that $\alpha$, the stable disposition that we call risk sensitivity, is normally distributed in a population. On the contrary, $\alpha_n$ will be distributed around the objective risk value. Suppose that violations of the norm that one should wait in line when paying at the supermarket are relatively well known to elicit a strong display of disapproval. In this case, most people's $\alpha_n$ will cluster around the typical disapproval response.

Figures 5.1 through 5.3 illustrate how the independent factors ă and $k_n$ could predict how likely one is to switch from an established norm to a new behavior. Figures 5.1, 5.2, and 5.3 show this interaction when no other members of the population have already switched to the new behavior, when 30 percent of the population have already switched, and when 55 percent of the population have switched, respectively. The higher an individual's ă, the more cautious she will be when deliberating whether to adopt a new behavior. A high-ă individual will want to wait and see how her peers fare after adopting a new behavior before adopting it herself, while a low ă individual will be more reckless in her decision-making. It is important to note that in the following Figures 5.1 through 5.3, I am not modeling how objective risks, which undoubtedly fluctuate in intensity and likelihood as more people adopt a new behavior, factor into one's decision to continue adhering to a norm.

Notice that with increasing abandonment of an old behavior, the distribution of ă that I model in Figures 5.1 through 5.3 significantly changes, precisely because there is usually a correlation (though imperfect) between real and perceived risks. As more and more people abandon a social norm, disobedience is perceived as increasingly less risky, and the curve that depicts the distribution of ă will come to reflect this change in perceived risks. It is important to note that the distribution of ă will not fluctuate as much as the distribution of $\alpha_n$ precisely because ă also takes into account the stable disposition α, which does not fluctuate from situation to situation.

Similarly, people who are very sensitive to a norm (i.e., those who have a high $k_n$), in that they think that the behavioral rule is important, will not look very favorably at alternatives. The society in which norm-sensitive individuals are embedded will have to undergo a sizable shift before they are willing to change behavior. As you can see from Figures 5.1 through 5.3, the distribution of $k_n$ stays constant across situations. I already noted that sensitivity ($k_n$) might change following the availability of new information that reliably signals that a practice may be damaging. In that case, $k_n$ may change as one reevaluates the importance of following that particular practice. This change in sensitivity should not depend on what other people do. Instead, it exemplifies the change in reasons that I consider to be a necessary condition for a change in behavior. Yet, I have chosen to keep the distribution of $k_n$ constant in Figures 5.1 through 5.3 to highlight the fact that, though ă will necessarily change as more people abandon a certain behavior (assuming abandonment is observable), the distribution of $k_n$ is not sensitive to social considerations, such as changing levels of abandonment.

I should also stress the fact that, given a specific and stable $k_n$, the likelihood of abandoning a practice will depend on one's empirical expectations (i.e., how many have abandoned it). People with a low $k_n$ will respond very quickly to a change in empirical expectations, while people with a high $k_n$ will need a dramatic shift in empirical expectations before being willing to change behavior. Those with a high $k_n$ have personal reasons that motivate them to adhere to a traditional practice that those with a low $k_n$ simply do not have. Because we are dealing with social norms, even the behavior of those with a very high $k_n$ is conditional and will eventually respond to changing social expectations, as the following figures show.

In Figure 5.1 below, where 0 percent of the population has deviated from a shared norm, even extremely norm insensitive individuals will factor into their decision-making how many of their peers have abandoned that practice.

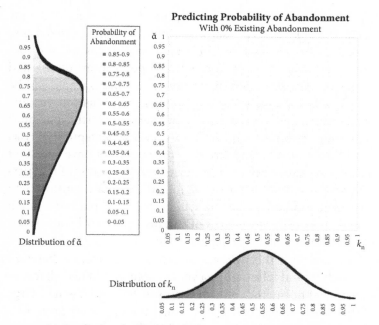

FIGURE 5.1 Predicting the likelihood of norm abandonment with varying distributions of risk sensitivity and risk perceptions (ă) and norm sensitivity ($k_n$), in the case of 0 percent abandonment.

What influences those individuals' choice will be their risk-sensitivity and situation-specific perceptions of risk (ă). As we can see, the low abandonment levels mean that a very low $k_n$ must be combined with a very low ă to induce an individual to abandon a social norm. It is the interaction of the right levels of ă and $k_n$ that enable someone to initiate social change. As I already mentioned, a trendsetter typically has both very low $k_n$ and low ă. Such trendsetters fall at the very extreme ends of both distributions of $k_n$ and ă, which means that only a very small segment of the population is willing to be the first to deviate from the established norm.

Let us now think of some possible situations that may occur in Figure 5.1. As I show in this figure, the ă distribution is skewed to the right precisely because there is usually (but not necessarily) a correlation between perceptions of risk and objective risks. The only "first movers" in this example will be people with extremely low ă and $k_n$. In this situation, imagine what someone with moderate $k_n$ and very low ă (this person is an extreme risk-taker and/or has a very low perception of risk) would do. Given his moderate $k_n$, he would not have sufficient reasons to change behavior because even the lowest of risk perceptions would not compensate for his moderate sensitivity to the norm. Similarly, a person with very low $k_n$ but moderate ă would fear the consequences of stirring the water by abandoning a norm that he may deeply dislike.

Figures 5.1 through 5.3 depict the difference between trendsetters and followers in a very simple way. When all follow a particular norm, the conformists' expected payoff will be large (either because of a high $k_n$ or because their ă is very large, or a combination of a moderate to low $k_n$ and a large ă), whereas the trendsetter's expected payoff for following the norm would be smaller (because of their lower sensitivity to the norm and low risk perception). It is also worth noting that the distribution of ă is changing through the figures because, as more and more people abandon the standing norm, objective risks and average risk perceptions are changing. This is reflected in the change in the distribution of ă.

Note that the change in shades in each graph, from light to deep gray, represents the probability of abandonment. In Figure 5.1, at the bottom left-hand corner of the graph where individuals have a low $k_n$ and a low ă, there is a small segment of dark gray. This shows that these individuals are likely to abandon a practice for the reasons that I have discussed. In this Figure, as ă and $k_n$ increase, the shades gradually become lighter, representing a decrease in the likelihood of abandonment.

In Figure 5.2 below, where 30 percent of the population has already abandoned a norm, we see that moderately norm-sensitive individuals (who were completely unwilling to abandon the practice when 0 percent of the population had abandoned it) are beginning to consider abandonment as a viable option.

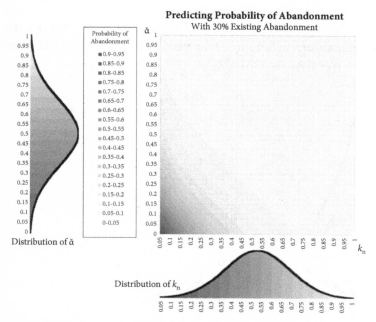

FIGURE 5.2 Predicting the likelihood of norm abandonment with varying distributions of risk sensitivity and risk perceptions ($\breve{a}$) and norm sensitivity ($k_n$), in the case of 30 percent abandonment.

Note that the distribution of $\breve{a}$ has significantly changed from the original distribution in Figure 5.1. Because a larger proportion of the population has abandoned the norm, the perceived risks of deviating have likely diminished (recall that ă is a combination of the stable trait of risk sensitivity and the more variable perception of risk). It should also be noticed that the distribution of $k_n$ has remained the same. However, the probability of norm abandonment of, say, a person with a $k_n$ of 0.3 has significantly increased, which is shown by the darker shade in the distribution of $k_n$ in Figure 5.2. This is true for every value of $k_n$ in this new distribution. Here we see that more moderate individuals, and not just trendsetters, are abandoning the norm.

Finally, in Figure 5.3 below, many more norm-sensitive individuals are willing to deviate from the established behavior than was the case initially.

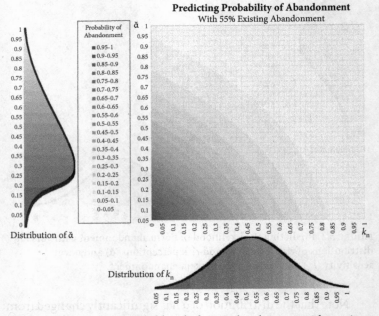

FIGURE 5.3 Predicting the likelihood of norm abandonment with varying distributions of risk sensitivity and risk perceptions (ă) and norm sensitivity ($k_n$), in the case of 55 percent abandonment.

Here, with 55 percent of the population abandoning the norm, there are slightly more people who are willing to deviate than there are people who are unwilling to deviate—this is the opposite of what we saw in Figure 5.1, where nobody had yet abandoned the norm. It appears that a tipping point has been reached. A tipping point is simply that point after which a population shifts from one behavior to another. In our case, a shift from one norm to another may be occurring, or people may simply abandon the current norm without adopting a new one. Notice that the distribution of ᾰ has again changed. This represents a further shift in people's perceptions of risk, since when a majority has abandoned a norm, the risks of deviating are considerably smaller than what they were initially. Similarly, the distribution of $k_n$ remains the same, but the probability of abandonment for each value of $k_n$ has substantially increased (as the darker shades show).

When identifying potential trendsetters in a population, it is important that their predictive traits (e.g., risk sensitivity/perception and norm sensitivity) are accurately measured. Here, the intervention designer should proceed with caution: not all psychological measurements are created equal (some are more accurate, reliable, or valid[13] than others), and they are often operationalized in different ways, as was the case with autonomy. Risk sensitivity ($\alpha$) is usually measured experimentally by looking at a range of individual decisions. Specific risk perceptions ($\alpha_n$) can be measured through surveys and vignettes where individuals are asked about what is likely to happen if a norm deviation occurs, varying the number of deviators.

13. Validity is an important consideration when designing a psychometric measurement. A measurement should be externally valid, in that it allows one to make inferences that extend beyond the study in question. It should also be internally valid in that it effectively taps into the phenomenon one is trying to address.

$k_n$ can be measured by presenting individuals with hypothetical scenarios in which we systematically induce different empirical and normative expectations and assess whether their behavior would change. The less it would change, the more sensitive one is to the particular norm.[14]

Once prospective trendsetters have been identified, interventions should target them first, because they have the highest likelihood of actually changing their behavior when no one else is willing. Beware that what I am showing here is just the simple dynamics of trendsetters and conformists. It is important to remember that we may face more extreme situations in which the distribution of $k_n$ with respect to a particular norm is not normal. For example, well-entrenched norms may be cherished by the population, thus showing a distribution of $k_n$'s that is skewed to the right. In such case, the likelihood of encountering a substantial number of trendsetters is low, and norm change will be unlikely to occur.

I am not arguing in this section that the process of social norm abandonment will be a fluid, progressive transition. Rather, I am showing how the likelihood of social norm abandonment will crucially depend on the distributions of the ă and $k_n$.

## THE DYNAMICS OF CHANGE

My goal in this section is not to provide a formal model of how change might occur, but instead to look at all the possible ways by which trendsetters may generate a change in social norms. In the previous section, I examined how the combination of norm sensitivity ($k_n$), risk sensitivity and risk

14. When using vignettes, we substitute hypothetical questions about the respondent with hypothetical situations about imaginary characters.

perception (ă) may lead people to deviate from a collective, interdependent practice (in the example, a social norm). Now I want to look more closely at how all of the important elements interact to jointly produce societal change. Of course, trendsetters live and act within a network of social relations. Consequently, the structure of this network may determine whether their deviant behavior will produce social change.

Let me reiterate the realistic assumption that there are different types of individuals with different psychological traits in a population. Specifically, individuals will have differing levels of risk sensitivity (a stable trait), norm-sensitivity, and risk-perception, as I mentioned in the previous section. The proportions of high and low ă and $k_n$ individuals in a population are not necessarily evenly distributed, and will likely vary from one norm to another. For example, it is unlikely that there would be just as many extremely norm-insensitive individuals in a population as there are moderately norm-sensitive individuals. The distribution of ă will depend, as I already mentioned, on the combination of normally distributed α's, a stable risk sensitivity trait, and a distribution of risk perceptions ($α_n$) that hovers around the measure of objective risk. An individual's type is, to a certain extent, situation-specific (in our case, norm-specific). A highly autonomous, self-efficacious, risk-insensitive individual might not be a trendsetter with respect to a particular norm. It would therefore be wrong to talk generically of "norm-entrepreneurs." Someone who is a trendsetter in abandoning child marriage may not be one in combatting corruption. It is only with respect to a specific norm that we can rank individuals' types according to their particular combination of $k_n$ and ă.

Depending on the distribution of these types in a population, change may or may not occur. Granovetter (1978; see also Braun 1995; Granovetter and Soong 1983, 1988) discusses how people have different thresholds for change, given their types.

Though my definition of types differs from Granovetter's, his discussion of thresholds still applies. In Granovetter's words, a threshold is "the number or proportion of others who must make one decision before a given actor does so; this is the point where net benefits begin to exceed the net costs for that particular actor" (1978, 1420). When behaviors are interdependent, it may be enough that 10 percent of people join a protest for an individual to follow suit, whereas a more conservative type will "wait and see" and join only when 80 percent of the population is participating. These individuals have very different thresholds—that is, the point at which they will change behavior. Some trendsetters will have a zero threshold, in the sense that they do not need to observe other early movers before engaging in counter-normative behavior. Their low sensitivity to a specific norm, accompanied by low ă, will lead them to deviate first. However, if there is a big gap between their threshold and other people's thresholds, no meaningful change is likely to occur.

Suppose we have five trendsetters who are willing to abandon a standing norm when none of their peers have abandoned it, and the rest of the relevant population is only willing to abandon when at least ten of their peers have abandoned.[15] In this case, no one else will follow the trendsetters, and the new behavior will die out. As Andrews and Biggs (2006) report, there were several sit-ins prior to the one in Greensboro, North Carolina that failed to incite the same rebellious fever. An important reason they mentioned was the low number of black college students prior to the 1960s. Even if all these students had a very low threshold for protest, there was a huge gap between them and the rest of the black population, who had much

15. Though in the previous figures I have presented distributions of ă and $k_n$ as continuous, it is certainly possible that discontinuous distributions exist.

more to lose and thus probably had a much higher threshold. However, this gap in thresholds may be filled if people assign different weights to the behavior of those around them. For example, the friends and family of the initial trendsetters will give more weight to their actions than strangers will. In this way, the action of five is "multiplied" for those socially close to the early movers: the friends and family who follow them will fill the gap. This "filling of the gap," if widespread, can make a discontinuous distribution functionally continuous.

If we assume a normal distribution of types (and hence of thresholds), a model of change could assume that this progressive adoption of new behavior would reach a tipping point, where the adoption of the behavior becomes self-sustaining (Kadushin 2012). As Figure 5.4 below shows, this model of change is presented as an S-shaped curve, which has been successfully used to describe the spread of innovations. In this model, adoption of the new behavior may slowly increase until it hits a tipping point upon which adoption rates massively increase and later taper off (due to saturation).

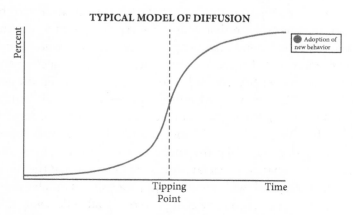

FIGURE 5.4 A graphic depiction of the S-shaped model of diffusion.

In the case of social norms, however, we do not usually observe the progressive adoption of a new behavior, but we instead see a sudden spike. Such spikes are by no means necessary. As we know from the Western experience during the '60s, traditional sexual mores and gender roles underwent a rapid change, but the change was not instantaneous, and it was experienced to varying degrees in different communities and across different generations. The advantage for my generation was that we could form networks that supported these changed standards, and allowed us the freedom to try new, alternative behaviors. By forming these independent networks, the price of deviance (if any) was not significant. I will come back to this important point later.

Often enough, however, individuals who want to change behavior face a social dilemma. If not enough people are changing, their change will be useless and, worse, penalized. I have already stressed the fact that the $k_n$ may not be normally distributed. Yet, whether the distribution of the $k_n$ is skewed to the right (most people are very sensitive to the norm) or to the left (most people are not very sensitive to the norm), there will be no change unless individuals are reasonably sure that they are not deviating alone. In the first case, sensitivity to the norm may be so high that people are very reluctant to deviate from it. In the second case, people's sensitivity to the norm may be very low, but if there is a mismatch between objective and perceived consensus, which is typical of pluralistic ignorance, risk perceptions may be extremely high, as most people believe that the norm is strongly endorsed by the population. In such cases, behavioral change is not gradual and continuous, and definitely does not take the shape of an S-curve. I have also argued that change in social norms, especially when the norm is well entrenched, will involve acquiring reasons for abandoning it. In this case, though a change in personal beliefs *may* take the form of an S-shaped curve, behavior will take a very different form, as I will show later.[16]

The 2011 protest in Tahrir Square that looked like a sudden spike in behavior was probably supported and preceded by a progressive change in personal beliefs that were not made overtly public (as discussion was probably limited to small groups of potential dissenters). There was a progressive accumulation of collective unrest and dissatisfaction with the old regime that found a voice in the Tahrir Square protest. As was the case with the Civil Rights Movement, the media played a critical role in disseminating information that the uprising was happening. Additionally, the very act of protesting is a costly signal powerful enough to convey the idea that dissenters are committed to change. In this case, the progressive change in personal normative beliefs (e.g., *we should not be silenced*) and the updating of normative/empirical expectations (facilitated by the media) came to a point at which people became sufficiently motivated to seek to coordinate a collective change.[17] A continuous, progressive change in personal beliefs is now accompanied by a discontinuous shift (or series of shifts) in behavior.

I have listed the media as a crucial tool for behavioral change. In the case of Tahrir Square, we are not talking about soap operas, but rather of the possibility of being informed about a change in behavior as it happens in real time. It is not only important to know that deviant behavior exists but, at the same time, to know that thousands of people who watch television or listen to the radio are aware that this change is occurring. Not only are we made aware of the uprising, but it stimulates discussion about the reasons and consequences of

16. If a majority of individuals have a high $k_n$, belief change will probably be slow. Depending on the mechanisms that induce this belief change, the curve that represents personal belief change in the target group at the time may not take the usual, smooth S-shape.

17. The updating of social expectations is often not so smooth.

this new behavior, unearthing people's true beliefs and feelings about their government. Dictatorships often exercise a tight control over the media largely because of this risk.

## GROUPS AS TRENDSETTERS

The most difficult problem to tackle in changing a social norm, as I already mentioned, is when people (though aware of alternatives) are uncritical of their standing practices. If there are dissidents, or if some community members can become convinced that their practices are harmful, then it may be possible for these individuals to come together into small groups. A possible vehicle of change here is the formation of small groups of trendsetters who change their own rules. If these groups can be self-sufficient, they can break off from the broader network in which they were previously embedded and create their own independent reference network. Think of the Amish, who came to America precisely because they rejected life in European society and wanted to create groups with their own rules and religion. They have remained independent and self-sufficient for centuries. These networks possess several prominent properties. They are dense and display a high level of homophily.[18] It is important to note that these networks did not spread their lifestyle to other nearby groups, nor did they want to. In fact, the Amish form a tightly knit group that is sufficiently segregated from the rest of society so as to impede diffusion.

In many cases, however, creating an independent network may not work. Take the case of marriageability: if marriage market norms encourage exogamous marriages, a local change

18. Density is usually measured as the average number of connections per node, whereas homophily means that similar individuals tend to be linked to each other (see Kadushin 2012).

in personal beliefs (both factual and normative) will not be sufficient to change marriage patterns. In this case, the reference network includes other communities of potential mates, and all these communities need to be involved for change to occur. A small group that wants to implement a new type of behavior (for example, ending child marriage or female genital cutting) will have an incentive to diffuse its new knowledge and convince other cohorts that change is necessary and worthwhile. Think of a small group that finds good reasons to abandon a given practice, such as female genital cutting, which is often a societal prerequisite for finding a husband. Suppose, further, that there are many communities of potential mates where this change has not occurred and will therefore need to be involved. In his study of foot binding in China, Mackie (1996) shows how organizing "natural foot societies," in which families committed to not bind their daughters' feet and allowed their sons only to marry unbound women, fought one of the main obstacles to the elimination of foot binding: the marriageability problem.[19] After a few trendsetters have started to form small networks, new members will need to have adequate incentives for joining. In China, marriage societies for the mutual abandonment of foot binding provided suitable mates for unbound girls. Being part of these networks changed members' empirical and normative expectations, thus creating a new marriage market. Of course, public campaigns were conducted to spread information about the adverse health effects of foot binding so as to provide families with reasons to

19. Prior to the advent of these natural foot societies, bound feet signaled chastity and gentility, despite their debilitating consequences for women's feet (Mackie 1996). As is the case now with FGC in many societies, it was originally difficult for a woman with unbound feet to find a good husband. When its prevalence was measured in 1835 (before the natural foot societies were started), 50 to 80 percent of Chinese women had their feet bound, with only women in the poorest communities having unbound feet.

end the practice. In my opinion, the most important element of change was the creation of separate networks that could eventually become self-sustaining. Creating networks of similarly motivated people will mitigate the effects of abandoning a shared practice. Indian non-dowry matrimonial websites[20] are another example of an attempt to create such "protected networks."

These initially small groups might need to recruit other cohorts in order to diffuse and sustain novel behavior. We may think of the starting group as a sort of collective trendsetter that wants to spread its new ideas to other networks. But how does the "collective trendsetter" successfully reach these other networks? Mackie and LeJeune (2009) discuss how diffusion of deliberation out of what they call the "core group" gets organized and, depending on the local culture, how this diffusion may work through local and more general networks. There are several possible channels of diffusion that may be employed: discussion with family and friends, meeting with elders, religious leaders, women groups, community meetings and discussions with nearby communities; or inter-village meetings with delegates from surrounding communities. All these interventions aim to secure a collective shift of personal beliefs (factual and normative) that could eventually facilitate a change in social expectations. Changing personal beliefs is not equivalent to changing social expectations, especially empirical ones. Changing the latter means either directly observing or trusting that a practice is being abandoned and that a new one is emerging. As I mentioned, the collective action problem may loom large in the sense that a change in personal beliefs, though shared with others, is not an assurance that behavior is changing. Acting alone is still risky.

20. For example, http://www.withoutdowry.com/, http://www.nodowry. net/, http://www.idontwantdowry.com/, and http://www.simplenikah. com/.

Even if a small, protected network were bent on changing certain practices, the problem of trust and commitment may still arise within the broader reference network. In the rare case in which the small group becomes independent from the rest of the network, it may be possible for it to self-support without needing to proselytize to others about the value of alternative behaviors. In this case, the isolationist group relies so much on itself that trust between members occurs naturally for the purpose of their own survival. Such groups will not need any formal or external signals of commitment. Recall the example of the Amish. For children who grow up in an Amish community, all they know is the lifestyle, values, and culture of their group, so leaving their community entails both a tremendous risk and a loss of identity. The small groups that decide to abandon a social norm that is shared in the wider population may not have the luxury of creating a self-sustaining independent network. For example, if female genital cutting is related to marriageability, and people usually marry in other villages, it becomes important to convince other villages to abandon the practice. Because of these circumstances, it may be difficult to be sure that one's group members will abandon the practice they have declared to be undesirable. Trust in the word of one's neighbors is important in this case.

One tool to build trust that change is indeed occurring is a public commitment—that is, promising to abandon the old practice and to adopt a new one. A public commitment may be very effective if it is done with people we know and with whom we have repeated interactions. We are motivated to stand by what we agree to, lest our reputation be tarnished. Nothing will convince others about the depth of our commitment like a costly signal. Another important advantage of public commitments is that a public declaration makes people resistant to opposing viewpoints. In communities where promises are honored, such commitments are a powerful tool to generate trust that change is coming. When we trust that other people will abandon an old practice and adopt a new one, we are functionally changing our empirical expectations about the future behavior of members of our reference network. Changing empirical expectations lessens the grip of normative ones, and actual change will follow. Many NGOs report witnessing massive public declarations where several villages pledged conformity to a new behavior. As a result, new normative expectations about how many members of one's reference network approved of the newly established behavior were created.

Public commitments, when successful, are an effective way to coordinate people's expectations that change will come. Other successful coordination mechanisms may be a trusted government mandate, or any visible, widely observable, and temporally specific form of commitment to change behavior. In this case, change may not be gradual. There will instead be a sudden spike in collective behavior. In Figure 5.5 below, we show a sudden spike in action combined with a much more gradual and continuous change in personal (normative) beliefs.

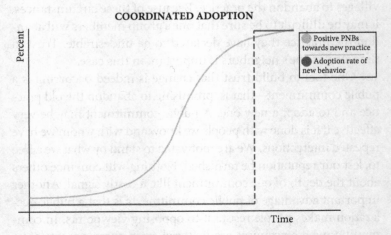

FIGURE 5.5 A graphic depiction of a society's sudden and complete adoption of a new practice, which is preceded by a gradual change in personal normative beliefs toward the practice.

Behavior does not change as smoothly because, in this particular situation, individuals want to be reasonably sure that their choice to abandon a standing norm will not be penalized. The spike therefore occurs when a mechanism that coordinates empirical expectations, and therefore actions, is in place.

Coordination, however, is rarely perfect. Either the message may not last long enough, or it may be heard by only a part of the population, or there may be some doubt about the legitimacy of the signal. An imperfect coordinating mechanism may induce part of the population to initiate new behavior, but this behavior, when of inadequate magnitude, may be too costly for people to sustain.

Figure 5.6 tells a common story of imperfect coordination. Like in Figure 5.5, the change in personal (normative) beliefs is gradual, whereas change in behavior is discontinuous. Change takes place at intervals that represent the working of coordinating mechanisms. We would thus observe a decline until some

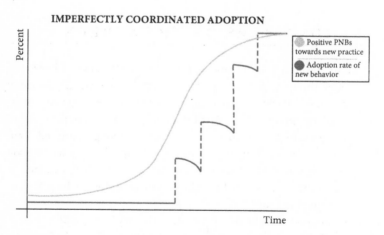

FIGURE 5.6 A graphic depiction of a society's progressive but discontinuous adoption of a new practice, which is preceded by a gradual change in personal normative beliefs toward the practice.

new coordinating device is implemented. In this respect, abandonment can be very fragile. This process may continue, with stops and starts, for a relatively long time until a large enough majority has moved along.

As in the case of the construction workers refusing to wear helmets that I mentioned earlier, an information campaign that explains the potential dangers of not wearing helmets on the job may have significantly changed workers' (factual and normative) beliefs about wearing helmets. Still, if wearing a helmet is an insult to a shared view of masculinity, change will be difficult to attain. The stepwise function I have depicted in Figure 5.6 may well represent how coordinating signals may induce some partial change. When the signal ends, even some who were convinced to wear helmets may revert to their old ways, realizing that not everyone coordinated on the signal. New, persistent signals will be needed to drive that population to a sustainable change.

## TRENDSETTERS ON THE SCREEN

I am old now and probably will not live much longer. I have seen many things in my life, but this TV is the most significant thing that has happened to our village ever. Our whole day is now organized around the TV. At first I did not want my son to get one, but now even I watch many hours of TV. Even though I am old, I am learning every day about many things. I hope that one day my son can have some of the things that we see on TV. We bought a fan last year for when it is very hot. All the people in the city have fans so we bought one too.

How do you know all the people in the city have fans?

Oh! I see it on TV. We learn many things from TV. (Johnson 2001, 155)

The creation of small networks, or the organized diffusion of new ideas, starting from small groups, may not be a feasible alternative when the communities are very large (e.g., in large cities). Scaling up some interventions proves to be quite difficult. I already discussed the importance of the media in norm change. As the quotation at the beginning of this paragraph (provided by an elderly Indian man who lived in a village where television had just recently been introduced) makes clear, the effects of television can be quite powerful, and its effects can extend well beyond a viewer's consumption patterns. Part of the reason that the media (soap operas in particular) can be so effective in changing behavior is because they can, in a sense, function as trendsetters. The main character of a story about education or child marriage may be a girl belonging to a very typical family with which people can easily identify. The novelty is that the girl has different aspirations; for example, she wants an education and maybe wants to marry for love. This fictitious character takes the place of a real trendsetter, and her fictional adventures can highlight the expected hurdles and triumphs that new behavior will likely encounter. The fact that many people all watch the same program and often discuss it is an important avenue for change.

The effect of television on identity and behavior has been well documented. Condon (1988) provides an excellent ethnographic analysis of the rapid effect of the introduction of television into an Inuit community. The Inuit have a traditionally collectivistic culture that condemns calling attention to personal triumphs. After having the opportunity to watch many hours of professional hockey and American sitcoms, Inuit adolescents not only began to play hockey, but they approached it with a competitive spirit and often bragged about their athletic prowess. They also began to openly express affection, an unusual behavior in traditional Inuit society that several adolescents attributed to watching the American show *Happy Days*. These adolescents began to integrate the lifestyles they saw broadcasted on television into their personal lives.

In India, young people similarly appear to learn about alternative lifestyles by watching television, particularly soap operas. Some girls have reported preferences for "love marriages" (as opposed to arranged marriages) specifically because of the lifestyles they saw on television. Jensen (2003, 192) quotes one girl as saying,

> I've always insisted that I've got to have the right man and I won't just be able to adjust to anyone. . . . There have been pressures, if I can call them that, from family, but I've . . . not given in to it. I won't do that ever because I know the situation now. . . . From the very beginning things foreign and imported were very glamorous to me. From those days onward [when I became familiar with things foreign], I was against having an [arranged] marriage. . . . Arranged marriages in India are becoming obsolete, I think. Because even now in [arranged marriages], girls and boys . . . talk to each other. They come to know each other. Perhaps the decision may not be theirs, because in some traditional households it's not theirs. But they should get to know each other. But as for me, I should [decide] and know him.

Exposure to alternative lifestyles portrayed in these soap operas and television shows serves to demonstrate that there are alternative ways of behaving. Indeed, as Jensen and Oster (2009) demonstrated, the advent of cable television access in India was associated with lower acceptance rates of spousal abuse, a diminished preference for sons, greater levels of female autonomy,[21] and diminished fertility rates. One possible mechanism by which these soap operas are changing preferences

---

21. Female autonomy levels were measured by levels of household decision-making by women.

and behavior is by changing the viewers' schemata (Bicchieri and McNally 2016). The representative yet rebellious characters not only deviate from established practices, but their deviance meets with great success. Thus, viewers may begin to expect that if they were to deviate, then they would meet with the same success. If the viewers do indeed perceive the television characters to be representative of real people or real situations (as is often the case; see Johnson 2001; Scrase 2002), then these characters fill the role of a highly publicized trendsetter.

As to gender roles, there are many examples of how television succeeds in reshaping them. Johnson (2001, 157) extensively quotes reports from Indian village men that refer to television as a driver for change. One man remarked how "since TV has come to our village women are doing less work than before. They only want to watch TV. So we [men] have to do more work. Many times I help my wife clean the house." Television, acting as a trendsetter, presents people with new models of behavior. It changes scripts and may encourage people to try different behaviors. The message is even more powerful because everybody knows that all their friends watch the same programs. Changing behavior, in this case, may be perceived as less risky and isolating.

The wide reach of the media, television in this case, brings many important social benefits for the watchers. As a villager reported,

> You know these people [referring to neighbors] we used to be close friends. Somehow they managed to become friends with the up-Sarpanch and now go to his house to watch TV every Sunday. We don't go because we are not welcome there. All they talk about is what they see on TV, and we are not very good friends now. I think they learn a lot from the TV. Also they meet many people at the up-Sarpanch's house and make good connections. It's all because of TV that they have improved their lives. They get more jobs now because of all the people they talk to. (Johnson 2001, 161)

In this example, the introduction of television served to reconstruct the village's social network, and the creation of new connections led to new job opportunities.

Though dramatic television productions can certainly have unintended effects on the lives of their viewers, some governments and international organizations have attempted to harness the power of entertainment to produce meaningful social changes. Such productions are often termed education-entertainment or "edutainment." One of the earliest edutainment productions, *Simplemente María* (*Simply María*), was produced in Peru and offered an alternate "rags-to-riches" reality of a young woman who successfully achieved upward social mobility through hard work and learning to read (Singhal, Obregon, and Rogers 1995). Though the educational effects of *Simplemente María* were unintended, their effects were very real: enrollment in adult literacy classes grew in Peru and surrounding countries, maids rose in social status (likely because the star of the show was a maid), and sales of sewing machines (which María frequently used) mushroomed.

Following the success of *Simplemente María*, many edutainment shows were put into production across Latin America (and eventually around the world) with the avowed intention to produce behavioral change. When they are well-designed, edutainment productions can essentially provide a tutorial for social change: through a vicarious reproduction of what effective change can look like, they demonstrate to viewers what they "should" expect when engaging in particular scripts (Bandura 2004). When the characters deviate from the socially prototypical behavioral paths, they typically meet with success, thus signaling to the viewers that, if they were to do the same, they would meet with the same success. This process likely amplifies the viewers' perceived self-efficacy, making them more willing to deviate. These televised behavioral models are relevantly similar to those that frustrated the

Indian men quoted by Johnson (2001), which I refer to earlier in this section.

The broadcasting of *Tinka Tinka Sukh* (*Happiness Lies in Small Things*), an Indian radio soap designed to promote equality and female empowerment, resulted in a particularly powerful influence in the village of Lutsaan (Singhal and Rogers 1999). Leaders of the village sent a large poster letter signed by 184 of its residents proclaiming that "listening to *Tinka Tinka Sukh* has benefited all listeners of our village, especially the women.... Our village now actively opposes the practice of dowry" (Singhal and Rogers 1999, 1). The show had such an impact on some of the residents that one particularly invested tailor even claimed that the show had completely changed his life:

> For the past ten years I lost my way, but *Tinka Tinka Sukh* showed me a new path of life. . . . I used to be delinquent, aimless, and a bully. I harassed girls. . . . One girl reported me to the police, and I was sent to prison. I came home unreformed. One day I heard a program on radio. . . . After listening to the drama, my life underwent a change. . . . One day I learned that *Tinka Tinka Sukh*, a radio soap opera, will be broadcast from AIR, Delhi. I waited expectantly. Once I started listening to the radio program, all my other drawbacks and negative values were transformed. (Singhal and Rogers 1999, 1)

As in the case of *Twende na Wakati*, which I discussed in the previous chapter in the Media Campaigns section, *Tinka Tinka Sukh* provided its listeners with clear examples of what happens when they engage in particular lifestyles (Singhal and Rogers 1999). Child marriage resulted in a death through childbirth, and a bride's "inadequate" dowry resulted in extreme mistreatment by her husband's family. Eventually, the characters signal disapproval for these norms (thus showing a low $k_n$), and reject them in favor of more progressive practices. Personal and collective efficacy are also stressed: several of the show's initially negative characters are able to abandon their vices and direct their lives in healthier directions. The tailor who is quoted above claimed that he was able to change his ways precisely because a disreputable character in the show was able to reform, demonstrating to him that change is possible. The success that these characters meet with, and the surmountable tribulations that they encounter, signal to the viewer that the risks associated with abandoning such norms are manageable. These signals can help reduce the viewers' perceptions of risk, thus making them more willing to deviate themselves. At the same time, the viewer's sensitivity to the standing norm ($k_n$) undergoes change by a process of learning about all the negative consequences of such practices.

Beyond anecdotal evidence, these positive models prompted the Lutsaan village to make sweeping changes. For example, in the course of the show's broadcast, the ratio of boys to girls in school transformed from 90:10 to 60:40, largely due to the influence of the show.

Miguel Sabido, the arguable "father" of edutainment productions, actually designed his shows to have characters who behave in a way that provides concrete "instructions" for particular adaptive behaviors (Bandura 2004). For example, in his production *Ven Conmigo* (*Come with Me*), which was designed to encourage literacy in its viewer base, the characters took advantage of actual governmental programs to learn to read. The show employed motivational epilogues after each episode that featured dramatic music, outlined the tangible benefits of certain behaviors, and provided specific instructions for how to take advantage of particular programs. For example, after one epilogue encouraged the viewers to enroll in a literacy program, "about 25,000 people descended on the distribution center in downtown Mexico City to obtain their reading materials! The resulting traffic jam tied up vehicles for many hours" (Bandura 2004, 89–90). Over the course of the year when the show was televised, a total of 839,943 individuals enrolled in adult literacy and education classes, representing a ninefold increase in enrollments over the previous year (Singhal and Rogers 1991).

In addition to promoting literacy, these productions have been designed to combat gender inequality, spousal abuse, unhealthy sexual practices, and many other maladaptive behaviors (see, e.g., Bandura 2004; Brown 1992; Rogers et al. 1999). For example, in India, the soap opera *Hum Log* (*We People*) was designed to reduce gender inequality and stem population growth (Singhal and Rogers 1991; Singhal and Rogers 1999). As was the case in *Ven Comigo, Hum Log* presented viewers with an epilogue (voiced by the show's father figure,[22] Kumar) at the end of each episode, often questioning a particular practice or value, and encouraged viewers to send in letters with their thoughts. For example, at the end of one particular episode, Kumar encouraged viewers to question traditional gender roles by asking, "Is the role of women restricted to the household or should it go beyond?" and prompting them to mail in their thoughts (Singhal and Rogers 1999, 84).

*Hum Log* attracted an unprecedentedly large viewer base that collectively sent in hundreds of thousands of letters in response to the epilogues. Analyses of these letters showed that audience members' personal normative beliefs appeared to be positively influenced by the show and that they felt deeply connected[23]

22. It was intentional that the show's father figure was chosen to read the epilogues. In India, learning from elders is a cherished value, and so Kumar had the strongest chance at being convincing. The strategy appeared to be effective, as many of the viewers addressed Kumar as "dada" or "grandfather" in their letters (Singhal and Rogers 1999).

23. Again, as I discussed in the section of chapter 3 that addresses scripts and schemata, it is important that viewers feel personally connected to a show's characters in order for the show to carry a substantial influence.

to the characters. Indeed, many young girls and boys wrote to Kumar, begging him to convince their parents to let them marry the person of their choice (Singhal and Rogers 1999). One particular village sent a large poster, signed by its residents, promising that they would end dowry practices and stop child marriages (Bandura 2004). Similarly to the earlier example of *Tinka Tinka Sukh*, enrollment rates of girls in elementary school rose from 10 percent to 38 percent in just one year of *Hum Log*'s broadcast.

Beyond offering motivational information and presenting characters that functionally serve the role of trendsetters, these edutainment productions (when well-designed) also serve to make new messages morally coherent with the existing local moral structure (Brown, Singhal, and Rogers 1989). Just as discussions can serve to reorganize the existing mental associations between particular morally laden concepts, these dramas can reconfigure a potentially contentious concept in a benign and even positive light (Bandura 2004). Indeed, some of Sabido's productions that promoted family planning in Mexico (such as *Acompaname* or *Accompany Me*) were initially met with resistance, but eventually that resistance gave way to support when the idea of family planning was "presented concretely in a value matrix" and framed as being supportive of existing values, such as health and dignity (Bandura 2004, 87). Indeed, despite this initial resistance, there was a 33 percent increase in Mexican visits to family planning clinics to obtain contraceptives while the show was on the air (Singhal and Rogers 1991). To ensure that the production is achieving the aforementioned goals, the producers typically monitor how viewers react to it and with which characters they identify.

In sum, soap operas and other media-based narratives have the potential to change much more than just scripts and schemata (which I discussed in the Media Campaigns section of chapter 4). They can change individuals' sensitivity to a norm ($k_n$) either by directly explaining the merits of alternative practices or by vicariously demonstrating their merits through the actions of fictitious characters. They can also signal that deviating from particular norms is not as risky as the viewer might think (thus lowering $\alpha_n$, and by extension, $\breve{a}$) and that change is possible (thereby improving viewers' perceived self-efficacy). Because people watch these shows together (and because they can reasonably infer that others are watching it elsewhere), people may update their normative expectations. That is, if a viewer is convinced by a soap opera that a practice should be stopped, then she might infer that other viewers are similarly updating their personal normative beliefs.[24] What may be particularly effective about these soap operas is that they typically feature characters who are representative of all major social groups (rich, poor, mother, father, child, teacher, etc.). The fact that the shows portray members of all walks of life coming together to condemn a practice signals that many elements of the viewers' reference networks may also be aware of the problems associated with a practice, and that they might be willing to fight it.

Together, the personal and social belief changes resulting from the influence of soap operas and edutainment have the potential to speed along the process of norm abandonment. Having a newly diminished $\breve{a}$ and $k_n$, greater perceived self-efficacy, and the new normative expectation that others do not approve of a practice, will all serve to make individuals more willing to deviate from a norm. Bandura (2004, 94) even argues that, in principle, "through the socially mediated path of influence, televised modeling can set in motion an ever-widening, reverberating process of social change." If perfectly coordinated abandonment is not necessary, then people will abandon a social norm at a faster rate than they would otherwise (this is assuming that the production

---

24. Experimental work on the effects of soap operas (Paluck 2009) has confirmed that they can indeed update viewers' or listeners' social expectations.

stays on the air until norm abandonment has reached a tipping point). Sending girls to school or changing breastfeeding practices are examples of situations where change does not require full participation. Instead, if abandoning a norm calls for strong coordination, coordination may be attainable at an earlier point in time. In fact, some shows could even provide viewers with such coordinating signals: for example, some of the epilogues in Sabido's soap operas actually instructed viewers to take advantage of specific governmental programs at particular points in time (Bandura 2004). Now, these epilogues were tackling adult literacy, which does not require coordinated action, but the same type of signals could be used to coordinate viewers' actions in other instances where coordination is necessary.

How do the effects of these productions change over time? Keeping the show on the air for a longer period of time has been shown to lead to increased effects, though at a diminishing rate. For example, as *Twende na Wakati* was broadcasted for a long time, the rate at which people visited family planning clinics to obtain contraception gradually rose, but it rose at an increasingly slow pace. Unfortunately, there are few analyses that look at the effectiveness of edutainment productions over time (instead, they look at their effectiveness as compared to control years), and there is limited data available to comment on the sustainability of their effects after the program goes off the air. In fact, some experts on edutainment have acknowledged that investigations into the long-term effects of edutainment on a population are rarely carried out and that they should be in the future (Singhal, Cody, Rogers, and Sabido 2003; Tufte 2001).

## FINAL THOUGHTS

As you can see, changing social norms is particularly complex because of their nature. They involve a normative component, and transgressions are usually socially sanctioned. Abandoning norms requires a major shift in empirical expectations: we have to be sure that many others are changing their ways in order to move away from an established norm. With a major shift in empirical expectations, the normative expectations that support a norm weaken to the point of collapse.

I have also stressed the importance of having reasons for change. Here the difference between descriptive norms (for example conventions) and social norms is evident. To change a convention, the most important thing to change are individuals' expectations about other people's behavior. The only reason to change behavior is the expectation that other people in one's reference network are also changing. No additional reasons are needed. Social norms are grounded on conditional preferences, too, but they also entail normative expectations. Recall that normative expectations are second-order normative beliefs. They are beliefs about what most members of our reference network think one should do. For successful abandonment to happen, we must be sure that the normative beliefs of those who matter to us are changing. If we know that others' normative beliefs are now different, our normative expectations will change too.

Especially with well-established norms, many followers have developed personal reasons to obey them. These reasons are not just dictated by prudence, and they have to change to set off the process of norm change. Those with low sensitivity to a norm will mostly pay attention to the proportion of people who are changing behavior. But individuals who are highly sensitive to a norm will need to be convinced that the norm is harmful or inefficient. Even so, we must realize that, to abandon a social norm, social expectations also need to change: I may become convinced that a norm is harmful, but fear of the consequences of nonconformity may hold me back.

Because a social norm is embedded in a thick web of beliefs, values, and other norms, working to change the reasons for conforming to a norm will involve working on the scripts and schemata of those who hold it. Changing cognitive scripts is not a linear, simple process: we often react to new information by "sanitizing" it, usually via subtyping. The bookkeeping model of change is the most successful, but it requires long-term, consistent exposure to examples of alternative behaviors. Soap operas, especially those that last a long time, exemplify the "bookkeeping" change. Personal belief change may be represented by an S-shaped curve, and may be more or less smooth, depending on the original distribution (normal or skewed) of the $k_n$, the degrees of allegiance to the norm, in the target population.

As opposed to personal belief change, I have argued that behavioral change will generally not be gradual. Assuming that people have acquired sufficient personal reasons for change, most individuals may not change for fear of the negative consequences of solitary deviance (or even small group deviance, when the deviant group cannot be independent). Trendsetters are the exception, but there is no guarantee that the change they spearhead will be successful. Once individuals have the assurance that others will move alongside them, they will be willing to abandon the norm as a group. Here the change will be quite sudden. The point at which change takes place is a point of complete or partial coordination. Coordination mechanisms may vary. I have listed collective commitments, soap operas that reach large populations and induce collective discussions, governmental mandates, and widespread diffusion of trusted information about how much people's beliefs have changed as examples of potential coordination mechanisms.

Change, however, must start somewhere. Trendsetters, who can usually be identified by their low risk sensitivity, low risk perception, low allegiance to the standing norm, high autonomy, and high perceived self-efficacy, play a crucial role in initiating it. Even in the case of sudden change, a group of trendsetters who spearhead new behavior may have sent a collective signal to an already prepared population that change is occurring. I have discussed how trendsetters may be individuals, small networks, or even the media. In every case, they provide a model that change can occur or is already occurring, thus inducing more timid followers to take action.

The hardest part of norm change is the beginning. Few are willing to take risks to abandon established practices. We want to identify those few who are least afraid of taking risks and least tied to the norm. There are a few good measures of the general characteristics that trendsetters are likely to have, but only some of them are predictive of behavior in specific situations. Psychometric measures of autonomy and self-efficacy, as well as utility measures of risk sensitivity, do not tell us how a person will behave in a particular situation. Norm sensitivity and risk perception with respect to a norm are more predictive, since they are measured by assessing and systematically varying social expectations (and punishment chances) to determine if and how much expectations of others' behavior, normative beliefs and willingness to punish deviations matter to choice in a specific situation. The survey and vignette methods I have proposed can identify individuals who possess "trendsetter potential" among large groups with modest financial cost. Interventions that engage potential trendsetters will more likely succeed in leading to successful and sustainable social change.

# BIBLIOGRAPHY

Aguirre, K., O. Becerra, S. Mesa, and J. Restrepo. 2005. "Assessing the Effect of Policy Interventions on Small Arms Demand in Bogotá, Colombia." Background paper (unpublished). Centro de Recursos para el Análisis de Conflictos (CERAC), Bogotá. Geneva: Small Arms Survey.

Ajzen, I. 1991. "The Theory of Planned Behavior." *Organizational Behavior and Human Decision Processes* 50 (2): 179–211.

Ajzen, I., D. Albarracín, and R. Hornik, eds. 2007. *Prediction and Change of Health Behavior: Applying the Reasoned Action Approach.* Mawah, NJ: Lawrence Erlbaum Associates, Inc.

Ajzen, I., and M. Fishbein. 1977. "Attitude-Behavior Relations: A Theoretical Analysis and Review of Empirical Research." *Psychological Bulletin* 84 (5): 888–918.

Aldashev, G., I. Chaara, J. P. Platteau, and Z. Wahhaj. 2012. "Using the Law to Change the Custom." *Journal of Development Economics* 97 (2): 182–200.

Aldashev, G., J. P. Platteau, and Z. Wahhaj. 2011. "Legal Reform in the Presence of a Living Custom: An Economic Approach." *Proceedings of the National Academy of Sciences* 108 (Supplement 4): 21320–25.

Allcott, H., and S. Mullainathan. 2010. "Behavioral Science and Energy Policy." *Science* 327 (5970): 1204–5.

Amabile, T. M., W. DeJong, and M. R. Lepper. 1976. "Effects of Externally Imposed Deadlines on Subsequent Intrinsic Motivation." *Journal of Personality and Social Psychology* 34 (1): 92–98.

Andrews, K. T., and M. Biggs. 2006. "The Dynamics of Protest Diffusion: Movement Organizations, Social Networks, and News Media in the 1960 Sit-Ins." *American Sociological Review* 71 (5): 752–77.

Aronson, J., D. M. Quinn, and S. J. Spencer. 1998. "Stereotype Threat and the Academic Underperformance of Minorities and Women." In *Prejudice: The Target's Perspective*, edited by J. K. Swim and C. Stangor, 83–103. San Diego: Academic Press.

Bajaj, M. 2011. "Teaching to Transform, Transforming to Teach: Exploring the Role of Teachers in Human Rights Education in India." *Educational Research* 53 (2): 207–21.

Bandura, A. 1993. "Perceived Self-Efficacy in Cognitive Development and Functioning." *Educational Psychologist* 28 (2): 117–48.

———. 2004. "Social Cognitive Theory for Personal and Social Change by Enabling Media." In *Entertainment-Education and Social Change: History, Research, and Practice*, edited by A. Singhal, M. J. Cody, E. M. Rogers, and M. Sabido, 75–96. Mahwah, NJ: Lawrence Erlbaum Associates, Inc.

Berkowitz, A. D. 2005. "An Overview of the Social Norms Approach." In *Changing the Culture of College Drinking: A Socially Situated Health Communication Campaign*, edited by L. Lederman, L. Stewart, F. Goodhart, and L. Laitman, 193–214. New York: Hampton Press.

Berkowitz, A. D., and H. W. Perkins. 1987. "Current Issues in Effective Alcohol Education Programming." In *Alcohol Policies and Practices on College and University Campuses*, edited by Joan Sherwood, 69–85. Columbus, OH: National Association of Student Personnel Administrators Monograph Series.

Bernstein, L. 1992. "Opting Out of the Legal System: Extralegal Contractual Relations in the Diamond Industry." *The Journal of Legal Studies* 21 (1): 115–57.

Bicchieri, C. 1988. *Ragioni per credere, ragioni per fare: Convenzioni e vincoli nel metodo scientifico*. Milano: Feltrinelli Editore.

———. 2006. *The Grammar of Society: The Nature and Dynamics of Social Norms*. New York: Cambridge University Press.

———. 2010. "Norms, Preferences, and Conditional Behavior." *Politics, Philosophy and Economics*, 9 (3): 297–313.

———. 2012. Diagnostic process of identifying collective behaviors. *Social Norms, Social Change*. Penn-UNICEF Lecture, July

———. 2014. "Norms, Conventions and the Power of Expectations." In *Philosophy of Social Science*, edited by N. Cartwright, 208–29. Oxford: Oxford University Press.

Bicchieri, C., and A. Chavez. 2010. "Behaving as Expected: Public Information and Fairness Norms." *Journal of Behavioral Decision Making* 23 (2): 161–78.

———. 2013. "Norm Manipulation, Norm Evasion: Experimental Evidence." *Economics and Philosophy* 29 (2): 175–98.

Bicchieri, C., and J. Duffy. 1997. "Corruption Cycles." *Political Studies* 45 (3): 477–95.

Bicchieri, C., J. W. Lindemans, and T. Jiang. 2014. "A Structured Approach to a Diagnostic of Collective Practices." *Frontiers in Psychology* 5 (1418): 1–13.

Bicchieri, C., and A. Marini. 2016. "Ending Female Genital Cutting: The Role of Macro Variables." Working Paper, Behavioral Ethics Lab, University of Pennsylvania.

Bicchieri, C., and P. K. McNally. 2016. "Shrieking Sirens: Schemata, Scripts, and Social Norms: How Change Occurs." *Social Philosophy & Policy* 35 (1): forthcoming.

Bicchieri, C., and H. Mercier. 2013. "Self-Serving Biases and Public Justifications in Trust Games." *Synthese* 190 (5): 909–22.

———. 2014. "Norms and Beliefs: How Change Occurs." In *The Complexity of Social Norms*, edited by M. Xenitidou and B. Edmonds, 37–54. Dordrecht: Springer International Publishing.

Bicchieri, C., and R. Muldoon. 2011. "Social Norms." *The Stanford Encyclopedia of Philosophy*, edited by E. N. Zalta. http://plato.stanford.edu/archives/spr2014/entries/social-norms/.

Bicchieri, C., and E. Xiao. 2009. "Do the Right Thing: But Only If Others Do So." *Journal of Behavioral Decision Making* 22 (2): 191–208.

Bicchieri, C., E. Xiao, and R. Muldoon. 2011. "Trusting Is Not a Norm, but Reciprocity Is." *Politics, Philosophy and Economics* 10 (2): 170–87.

Bicchieri, C., and J. Zhang. 2012. "An Embarrassment of Riches: Modeling Social Preferences in Ultimatum Games." In *Handbook of the Philosophy of Science*, vol. 13, *Philosophy of Economics*, edited by U. Maki, 577–95. Amsterdam: Elsevier.

Boudet, A. M., P. Petesch, C. Turk, and M. A. Tumala. 2012. On Norms and Agency. *The World Bank*.

Braun, N. 1995. "Individual Thresholds and Social Diffusion." *Rationality and Society* 7 (2): 167–82.

Brown, W. J. 1992. "Sociocultural Influences of Pro-development Soap Operas in the Third World." *Journal of Popular Film and Television* 19 (4): 157–64.

Brown, W. J., A. Singhal, and E. M. Rogers. 1989. "Pro-Development Soap Operas: A Novel Approach to Development Communication." *Media Development* 36 (4): 43–47.

Camerer, C., and E. Fehr. 2002. "Measuring Social Norms and Preferences Using Experimental Games: A Guide for Social Scientists." Working Paper no. 97, January. Institute for Empirical Research in Economics, University of Zurich.

Castelli, I., D. Massaro, C. Bicchieri, A. Chavez, and A. Marchetti. 2014. "Fairness Norms and Theory of Mind in an Ultimatum Game: Judgments, Offers, and Decisions in School-Aged Children." *PloSOne* 9 (8): e105024.

Chaudhury, N., J. Hammer, M. Kremer, K. Muralidharan, and F. H. Rogers. 2006. "Missing in Action: Teacher and Health Worker Absence in Developing Countries." *The Journal of Economic Perspectives* 20 (1): 91–116.

Chong, A., and E. La Ferrara. 2009. "Television and Divorce: Evidence from Brazilian Novelas." *Journal of the European Economic Association* 7 (2–3): 458–68.

Condon, R. G. 1988. *Inuit Youth: Growth and Change in the Canadian Arctic. Adolescents in a changing world*, Vol. 1. Piscataway, NJ: Rutgers University Press.

Crocker, J., S. T. Fiske, and S. E. Taylor. 1984. "Schematic Bases of Belief Change." In *Attitudinal Judgment*, edited by R. Eiser, 197–226. New York: Springer.

Crowne, D. P., and D. Marlowe. 1960. "A New Scale of Social Desirability Independent of Psychopathology." *Journal of Consulting Psychology* 24 (4): 349.

Curtis, V. 2013. *Don't Look, Don't Touch, Don't Eat: The Science Behind Revulsion*. Chicago: University of Chicago Press.

Dana, J., R. A. Weber, and J. X. Kuang. 2007. "Exploiting Moral Wiggle Room: Experiments Demonstrating an Illusory Preference for Fairness." *Economic Theory* 33 (1): 67–80.

Datta, S., and S. Mullainathan. 2012. "Behavioral Design: A New Approach to Development Policy." *CGD Policy Paper 016*. Washington, DC: Center for Global Development. http://www.cgdev.org/files/content/publications/detail/1426679.

Deci, E. L. 1971. "Effects of Externally Mediated Rewards on Intrinsic Motivation." *Journal of Personality and Social Psychology* 18 (1): 105–15.

Deci, E. L., and R. M. Ryan. 1985. "The General Causality Orientations Scale: Self-Determination in Personality." *Journal of Research in Personality* 19 (2): 109–34.

Deutsch, M., and H. B. Gerard. 1955. "A Study of Normative and Informational Social Influences upon Individual Judgment." *The Journal of Abnormal and Social Psychology* 51 (3): 629–36.

Diop, N. J., M. M. Faye, A. Moreau, J. Cabral, H. Benga, F. Cissé, B. Mane, I. Baumgarten, and M. Melching. 2004. *The Tostan Program: Evaluation of a Community Based Education Program in Senegal*. Washington, DC: Population Council.

Dolcini, M. M., L. Canin, A. Gandelman, and H. Skolnik. 2004. "Theoretical Domains: A Heuristic for Teaching Behavioral Theory in HIV/STD Prevention Courses." *Health Promotion Practice* 5 (4): 404–17.

Eagly, A. H., and S. Chaiken. 1993. *The Psychology of Attitudes*. Orlando, FL: Harcourt Brace Jovanovich College Publishers.

Elias, N. 1978. *The Civilizing Process: The History of Manners*. Oxford: Blackwell.

Falk, A., E. Fehr, and U. Fischbacher. 2003. "On the Nature of Fair Behavior." *Economic Inquiry* 41 (1): 20–26.

Fehr, E., and S. Gachter. 2000. "Cooperation and Punishment in Public Goods Experiments." *American Economic Review* 90 (4): 980–94.

Fehr, E., and U. Fischbacher. 2004. "Third-Party Punishment and Social Norms." *Evolution and Human Behavior* 25 (2): 63–87.

Feldner, Y. 2000. "'Honor' Murders—Why the Perps Get Off Easy." *Middle East Quarterly* 7 (4): 41–51.

Fenton-O'Creevy, M., E. Soane, and P. Willman. 2001. *Risk Propensity and Personality*. London: London Business School, Centre for Organizational Research.

Ferraro, P. J., J. J. Miranda, and M. K. Price. 2011. "The Persistence of Treatment Effects with Norm-Based Policy Instruments: Evidence from a Randomized Environmental Policy Experiment." *The American Economic Review* 101 (3): 318–22.

Festinger, L. 1962. *A Theory of Cognitive Dissonance*. Vol. 2. Stanford: Stanford University Press.

Finch, J. 1987. "The Vignette Technique in Survey Research." *Sociology* 21 (1): 105–14.

Fishbein, M. 1967. "A Consideration of Beliefs and Their Role in Attitude Measurement." In *Readings in Attitude Theory and Measurement*, edited by M. Fishbein, 477–92. New York: Wiley.

———. 2007. "A Reasoned Action Approach: Some Issues, Questions, and Clarifications." In *Prediction and Change of Health Behavior: Applying the Reasoned Action Approach*, edited by I. Ajzen, D. Albarracín, and R. Hornik, 281–95. Mahwah, NJ: Lawrence Erlbaum Associates.

Fishbein, M., and I. Ajzen 2011. *Predicting and Changing Behavior: The Reasoned Action Approach*. New York: Taylor and Francis.

Fiske, S., and S. Taylor. 1991. *Social Cognition*. New York: McGraw-Hill Book Company.

Fitzgerald, J., and J. Wolak. 2016. "The Roots of Trust in Local Government in Western Europe." *International Political Science Review* 37 (1): 130–46.

Fuller, C. J., ed. 1996. *Caste Today*. Oxford: Oxford University Press.

Gausset, Q. 2001. "AIDS and Cultural Practices in Africa: The Case of the Tonga (Zambia)." *Social Science and Medicine* 52 (4): 509–18.

Gillespie, D., and M. Melching. 2010. "The Transformative Power of Democracy and Human Rights in Nonformal Education: The Case of Tostan." *Adult Education Quarterly: A Journal of Research and Theory* 60 (5): 477–98.

Gneezy, U., S. Meier, and P. Rey-Biel. 2011. "When and Why Incentives (Don't) Work to Modify Behavior." *Journal of Economic Perspectives* 25 (4): 191–210.

Gneezy, U., and A. Rustichini. 2000. "A Fine Is a Price." *Journal of Legal Studies* 29 (1): 1–17.

Goldstein, N. J., R. B. Cialdini, and V. Griskevicius. 2008. "A Room with a Viewpoint: Using Social Norms to Motivate Environmental Conservation in Hotels." *Journal of Consumer Research* 35 (3): 472–82.

Granovetter, M. 1978. "Threshold Models of Collective Behavior." *American Journal of Sociology* 83 (6): 1420–43.

Granovetter, M., and R. Soong. 1983. "Threshold Models of Diffusion and Collective Behavior." *Journal of Mathematical Sociology* 9 (3): 165–79.

———. 1988. "Threshold Models of Diversity: Chinese Restaurants, Residential Segregation, and the Spiral of Silence." *Sociological Methodology* 18 (6): 69–104.

Greenberg, B. G., A. Abul-Ela, W. R. Simmons, and D. G. Horvitz. 1969. "The Unrelated Question Randomized Response Model: Theoretical Framework." *Journal of the American Statistical Association* 64 (325): 520–39.

Guala, F., and L. Mittone. 2010. "Paradigmatic Experiments: The Dictator Game." *The Journal of Socio-Economics* 39 (5): 578–84.

Guigui, M. T. 2012. "Improving Exclusive Breastfeeding Practices in Chad through Change in Social Norms." A Case Study for Learning Program on Advances in Social Norms and Implications for Programming." Penn-UNICEF Social Norms, Social Change Paper, July.

Hadi, A. A. 2006. "A Community of Women Empowered: The Story of Deir El Barsha." In *Female Circumcision: Multicultural Perspectives*, edited by R. M. Abusharaf, 104–24. Philadelphia: University of Pennsylvania Press.

Haile G. D., F. H. Meskal, and T. Teshome. 2004. Woman's Affairs Office in collaboration with the National Committee on Traditional Practices, Ethiopian Women Lawyers Association and UNICEF/Ethiopia: Nabling communities abandon harmful traditional practices, with special reference to female genital mutilation, early marriage, marriage by abduction and perinatal harmful traditional practices. Addis Ababa: UNICEF/Ethiopia.

Hampson, S. E., H. H. Severson, W. J. Burns, P. Slovic, and K. J. Fisher. 2001. "Risk Perception, Personality Factors and Alcohol Use among Adolescents." *Personality and Individual Differences* 30 (1): 167–81.

Henrich, J., R. Boyd, S. Bowles, C. Camerer, E. Fehr, H. Gintis, R. McElreath, M. Alvard, A. Barr, J. Ensminger, N. S. Henrich, K. Hill, F. Gil-White, M. Gurven, F. V. Marlowe, J. Q. Patton, and D. Tracer. 2005. "'Economic Man' in Cross-Cultural Perspective: Behavioral Experiments in 15 Small-Scale Societies." *Behavioral and Brain Sciences* 28 (6): 795–815.

Hill, D. 1971. "Peer Group Conformity in Adolescent Smoking and Its Relationship to Affiliation and Autonomy Needs." *Australian Journal of Psychology* 23 (2): 189–99.

Hmel, B. A., and A. L. Pincus. 2002. "The Meaning of Autonomy: On and Beyond the Interpersonal Circumplex." *Journal of Personality* 70 (3): 277–310.

Hoq, M. N. 2013. "Regional Differentials of Age at First Marriage among Women in Bangladesh." *Asian Journal of Applied Science and Engineering* 2 (2): 76–83.

Hume, D. 1738 (1882). *A Treatise of Human Nature.* London: Longmans, Green, & Co.

Jackson, J. 1965. "Structural Characteristics of Norms." In *Current Studies in Social Psychology*, edited by I. D. Steiner and M. Fishbein, 301–9. New York: Holt, Rinehard and Winston.

Jensen, L. A. 2003. "Coming of Age in a Multicultural World: Globalization and Adolescent Cultural Identity Formation." *Applied Developmental Science* 7 (3): 189–96.

Jensen, R. 2012. "Do Labor Market Opportunities Affect Young Women's Work and Family Decisions? Experimental Evidence from India." *The Quarterly Journal of Economics* 127 (2): 753–92.

Jensen, R., and E. Oster. 2009. "The Power of TV: Cable Television and Women's Status in India." *The Quarterly Journal of Economics* 124 (3): 1057–94.

Johnson, K. 2001. "Media and Social Change: The Modernizing Influences of Television in Rural India." *Media, Culture and Society* 23 (2): 147–69.

Jones, E. E., and V. A. Harris. 1967. "The Attribution of Attitudes." *Journal of Experimental Social Psychology* 3 (1): 1–24.

Kadushin, C. 2012. *Understanding Social Networks: Theories, Concepts, and Findings.* New York: Oxford University Press.

Kagel, J. H., C. Kim, and D. Moser. 1996. "Fairness in Ultimatum Games with Asymmetric Information and Asymmetric Payoffs." *Games and Economic Behavior* 13 (1): 100–110.

Kahan, D. 2000. "Gentle Nudges vs. Harsh Shoves: Solving the Sticky Norms Problem." *University of Chicago Law Review* 67: 607–45.

Knee, C. R., and C. Neighbors. 2002. "Self-Determination, Perception of Peer Pressure, and Drinking Among College Students." *Journal of Applied Social Psychology* 32 (3): 522–43.

Koestner, R., and G. F. Losier. 1996. "Distinguishing Reactive Versus Reflective Autonomy." *Journal of Personality* 64 (2): 465–94.

Ko Ko, C. 2013. "Perception on Corporal Punishment to Children— A Case Study for Learning Program on Advances in Social Norms and Implications for Programming." Penn-UNICEF Social Norms, Social Change Paper, July.

Krosnick, J. A., and Judd, C. M. 1982. "Transitions in Social Influence at Adolescence: Who Induces Cigarette Smoking?" *Developmental Psychology* 18 (3): 359–68.

Kunda, Z. 1990. "The Case for Motivated Reasoning." *Psychological Bulletin* 108 (3): 480–98.

La Ferrara, E., A. Chong, and S. Duryea. 2008. "Soap Operas and Fertility: Evidence from Brazil." *American Economic Journal: Applied Economics* 4 (4): 1–31.

Launiala, A. 2009. "How Much Can a KAP Survey Tell Us about People's Knowledge, Attitudes and Practices? Some Observations from Medical Anthropology Research on Malaria in Pregnancy in Malawi." *Anthropology Matters* 11 (1). http://www.anthropologymatters.com/index.php/anth_matters/article/view/31.

Macaulay, S. 1963. "Non-Contractual Relations in Business: A Preliminary Study." *American Sociological Review* 28 (1): 55–67.

Mackie, G. 1996. "Ending Footbinding and Infibulation: A Convention Account." *American Sociological Review* 61 (6): 999–1017.

Mackie, G., and J. LeJeune. 2009. "Social Dynamics of Abandonment of Harmful Practices: A New Look at the Theory." *Innocenti Working Paper: Special Series on Social Norms and Harmful Practices*, 2009-06.

McClelland, J. L., D. E. Rumelhart, and PDP Research Group. 1986. *Parallel Distributed Processing. Explorations in the Microstructure of Cognition*. Vol. 2. Cambridge, MA: MIT Press.

Mendelsohn, H. 1973. "Some Reasons Why Information Campaigns Can Succeed." *Public Opinion Quarterly* 37 (1): 50–61.

Mercier, H., and D. Sperber. 2011. "Why Do Humans Reason? Arguments for an Argumentative Theory." *Behavioral and Brain Sciences* 34 (2): 57–74.

Mellström, C., and M. Johannesson. 2008. "Crowding Out in Blood Donation: Was Titmuss Right?" *Journal of the European Economic Association* 6 (4): 845–63.

Milgram, S. 1992. *The Individual in a Social World: Essays and Experiments*. New York: McGraw-Hill Book Company.

Miller, D. T., and C. McFarland. 1987. "Pluralistic Ignorance: When Similarity Is Interpreted as Dissimilarity." *Journal of Personality and Social Psychology* 53 (2): 298.

Montaigne, M. de. 1580 (2003). *Michel de Montaigne: The Complete Essays*. Edited by M. A. Screech. London: Penguin Books. Can also be accessed from http://oll.libertyfund.org/title/1744/91226 on 2013-11-02.

Myers, D. G., and M. F. Kaplan. 1976 "Group Induced Polarization in Simulated Juries." *Personality and Social Psychology Bulletin* 2 (1): 63–66.

Nicholson, N., E. Soane, M. Fenton-O'Creevy, and P. Willman. 2005. "Personality and Domain-Specific Risk Taking." *Journal of Risk Research* 8 (2): 157–76.

Ostrom, E. 2009. "Design Principles of Robust Property-Rights Institutions: What Have We Learned?" In *Property Rights and Land Policies*, edited by G. K. Ingram and Y. Hong, 25–51. Cambridge, MA: Lincoln Institute of Land Policy.

Paluck, E. L. 2009. "Reducing Intergroup Prejudice and Conflict Using the Media: A Field Experiment in Rwanda." *Journal of Personality and Social Psychology* 96 (3): 574–87.

Parker, W., and M. B. Makhubele. 2010. *Threads of Violence against Women in South Africa: Findings from Community Surveys in the Western Cape and Kwazulu-Natal*. Cape Town, SA: Project Concern International.

Pascale, R., J. Sternin, and M. Sternin. 2010. *The Power of Positive Deviance: How Unlikely Innovators Solve the World's Toughest Problems*. Cambridge, MA: Harvard Business Press.

Payne, B. K. 2001. "Prejudice and Perception: The Role of Automatic and Controlled Processes in Misperceiving a Weapon." *Journal of Personality and Social Psychology* 81 (2): 181–92.

Platteau, J. P. 2000. Institutions, Social Norms, and Economic Development. Vol. 1. Mahwah, NJ: Psychology Press.

Rivis, A., and P. Sheeran. 2003. "Descriptive Norms as an Additional Predictor in the Theory of Planned Behaviour: A Meta-Analysis." *Current Psychology* 22 (3): 218–33.

Rogers, E. M., P. W. Vaughan, R. Swalehe, N. Rao, P. Svenkerud, and S. Sood. 1999. "Effects of an Entertainment-Education Radio Soap Opera on Family Planning Behavior in Tanzania." *Studies in Family Planning* 30 (3): 193–211.

Rosenthal, R. 1976. *Experimenter Effects in Behavioral Research*. New York: Irvington.

Ross, L. 1977. "The Intuitive Psychologist and His Shortcomings: Distortions in the Attribution Process." In *Advances in Experimental Social Psychology*. Vol. 10, edited by L. Berkowitz, 173–220. New York: Acedemic Press.

Rumelhart, D. E. 1998. "The Architecture of Mind: A Connectionist Approach." In *Mind Readings: Introductory Selections on Cognitive Science*, edited by P. Thagard, 207–38. Cambridge, MA: MIT Press.

Sanan, D., and S. G. Moulik. 2007. "Community-Led Total Sanitation in Rural Areas: An Approach that Works. Field notes." New Delhi, India: Water and Sanitation Program—South Asia.

Schopper, D., S. Doussantousse, and J. Orav. 1993. "Sexual Behaviors Relevant to HIV Transmission in a Rural African Population: How Much Can a KAP Survey Tell Us?" *Social Science and Medicine* 37 (3): 401–12.

Schultz, P. W., J. M. Nolan, R. B. Cialdini, N. J. Goldstein, and V. Griskevicius. 2007. "The Constructive, Destructive, and Reconstructive Power of Social Norms." *Psychological Science* 18 (5): 429–34.

Scrase, T. J. 2002. "Television, the Middle Classes and the Transformation of Cultural Identities in West Bengal, India." *International Communication Gazette* 64 (4): 323–42.

Shank, R. C., and R. P. Abelson. 1977. *Scripts, Plans, Goals, and Understanding: An Inquiry into Human Knowledge Structures*. Mahwah, NJ: Psychology Press.

Simmel, G. 1950. *The Sociology of Georg Simmel*. Toronto, ON: The Free Press.

Singhal, A., M. J. Cody, E. M. Rogers, and M. Sabido, eds. 2003. *Entertainment-Education and Social Change: History, Research, and Practice*. New York: Routledge.

Singhal, A., R. Obregon, and E. M. Rogers. 1995. "Reconstructing the Story of *Simplemente María*, the Most Popular Telenovela in Latin America of All Time." *International Communication Gazette* 54 (1): 1–15.

Singhal, A., and E. Rogers. 1991. "Hum Log Story: From Concept to After-Effects." *Communication 2000AD*. New Dehli: Indian Institute of Mass Communications, 17–25.

———. 1999. *Entertainment-Education: A Communication Strategy for Social Change*. Mahwah, NJ: L. Erlbaum Associates.

Slater, M. D. 2002. "Entertainment Education and the Persuasive Impact of Narratives." In *Narrative Impact: Social and Cognitive Foundations*, edited by M. C. Green, J. J. Strange, and T. C. Brock, 157–81. Mahwah, NJ: Erlbaum.

Snyder, M., E. D. Tanke, and E. Berscheid. 1977. "Social Perception and Interpersonal Behavior: On the Self-Fulfilling Nature of Social Stereotypes." *Journal of Personality and Social Psychology* 35 (9): 656.

Sorenson, S. B., and C. A. Taylor. 2005. "Female Aggression toward Male Intimate Partners: An Examination of Social Norms in a Community-Based Sample." *Psychology of Women Quarterly* 29 (1): 78–96.

Steele, C. M., and J. Aronson. 1995. "Stereotype Threat and the Intellectual Test Performance of African Americans." *Journal of Personality and Social Psychology* 69 (5): 797–811.

Stuntz, W. J. 2000. "Self-Defeating Crimes." *Virginia Law Review* 86 (8): 1871–99.

Stycos, J. M. 1981. "A Critique of Focus Group and Survey Research: The Machismo Case." *Studies in Family Planning* 12 (12): 450–56.

Tchibindat, F. 2012. "A Social Norms Perspective in Improving Infant Feeding in West and Central Africa: From Promoting Scientific Evidence to Addressing Factual Beliefs and Normative Expectations." A Case Study for Learning Program on Advances in Social Norms and Implications for Programming." Penn-UNICEF Social Norms, Social Change Paper, July.

Titmuss, R. 1970. *The Gift Relationship: From Human Blood to Social Policy.* New York: Random House.

Tufte, T. 2001. "Entertainment-Education and Participation: Assessing the Communication Strategy of Soul City." *Journal of International Communication* 7 (2): 25–50.

Tufte, T. 2004. "Telenovelas, Culture and Social Change: From Polisemy, Pleasure and Resistance to Strategic Communication and Social Development." In *International Perspectives on Telenovelas*, edited by M. Immacolata, 293–320. Sao Paulo: Edicoes Loyola and Re Globo.

Valdesolo, P., and D. DeSteno. 2008. "The Duality of Virtue: Deconstructing the Moral Hypocrite." *Journal of Experimental Social Psychology* 44 (5): 1334–38.

Watts, D. J. 2003. *Small Worlds: The Dynamics of Networks between Order and Randomness*. Princeton: Princeton University Press.

Weinstein, N., A. K. Przybylski, and R. M. Ryan. 2012. "The Index of Autonomous Functioning: Development of a Scale of Human Autonomy." *Journal of Research in Personality* 46 (4): 397–413.

Wicker, A. W. 1969. "Attitudes Versus Actions: The Relationship of Verbal and Overt Behavioral Responses to Attitude Objects." *Journal of Social Issues* 25 (4): 41–78.

Wishik, S. M., and S. Vynckt. 1976. "The Use of Nutritional 'Positive Deviants' to Identify Approaches for Modification of Dietary Practices." *American Journal of Public Health* 66 (1): 38–42.

Word, C. O., M. P. Zanna, and J. Cooper. 1974. "The Nonverbal Mediation of Self-Fulfilling Prophecies in Interracial Interaction." *Journal of Experimental Social Psychology* 10 (2): 109–20.

Xiao, E., and C. Bicchieri. 2010. "When Equality Trumps Reciprocity." *Journal of Economic Psychology* 31 (3): 456–70.

Yoder, P. S. 1995. "Examining Ethnomedical Diagnoses and Treatment Choices for Diarrheal Disorders in Lubumbashi Swahili." *Medical Anthropology* 16 (1–4): 211–47.

Zizzo, D. J. 2010. "Experimenter Demand Effects in Economic Experiments." *Experimental Economics* 13 (1): 75–98.

# INDEX

References to tables and figures should be denoted by an italic *t* or *f* following the page number.

norm manipulation, 80–81, 81n14
unconditional (social) preferences
  definition and examples, 7, 9t
  shared, 73

validity, 181, 181n13
vignettes, 103–104, 103n24
Viola, Franca, 76, 78

violation, social norms, 82–88,
  83n16. *see also* transgression
  evasion, 83, 83n16
  examples, 28–29, 29n11

Wahhaj, Z., 146

Xiao, Erte, 77, 86–87, 120